ADDING WOOD TO THE FIRE

A Quiltmaker's Way

ADDING WOOD TO THE FIRE

A Quiltmaker's Way

KATHY FORD

ROAD TO HOME PRESS

MASSACHUSETTS

For Molly and Ben

Contents

Quilt in process

Prologue: Adding Wood to the Fire

The morning isn't so cold. I don't need to build a fire to stay warm, but rather am called to build a ritual fire to do my sitting meditation. I pull the screen away from the open fireplace, crumple a few pieces of newspaper, throw on a pile of sticks gathered from the woods to use as kindling, retrieve a few thick stubs of wood from the ashes leftover from the last fire and place them gently on top. I light. Sit down on my cushion, arrange all my props for comfort in a cross-legged posture, put my arm around Nora who is leaning her sleek canine body into me, and watch the initial flare settle down before closing my eyes. It is an easy, peaceful meditation until I start focusing on the gentle snap and crackle of the flames. It isn't a big fire, just a small one that will last just so long, just long enough, I figure, before the timer will go off to signal the end of my sit. I love this little fire. I am settled and comfortable where I am sitting. I feel good. I spot another piece of charred wood in the back of the ashes. If I put that on top of this perfect little fire, it can keep going even longer, I can sit a little longer, I can prolong the joy.

I move to reach this other piece of wood. Once I place it on top and watch the flames slowly dissipate from the weight of the addition, I can't settle back into the perfectly comfortable position I have been in. The joy disappears. I watch with dismay as the fire actually fizzles out.

I think of all the places that fire manifests for me throughout a day. Not the actual, physical, orange-blue-flame kind in the fireplace, but the kind that starts in my belly and can spread warmth throughout body and soul. It is the fire that ignites when I begin to cook or start a new quilt. This is tantamount to rubbing two sticks together to get a flame. It takes hours, days, sometimes weeks to catch. Thoughts and images and feelings twirl for a good while before I am ready to begin putting pieces of fabric together. And then when I finally do, the fire ignites full orce, and I can't stop adding wood to the fire until there is something complete enough for me to stop and settle with.

I look at the pieces of fabric laid out on my dining room table, glowing embers now, and the decision before me is to add more or stay with what is here. I don't always stop when it might have been better if I had. The art of adding wood to the fire is about learning to stay. To stay just long enough. It requires discernment. It requires an intention to be in relation, to make a choice, and to yield. It is not meant to be done perfectly every time. It is about learning what it feels like to stay with self AND awareness at the same time, about allowing a partnership with what is to exist, if only for a moment, and maybe even illuminating a way to keep that partnership fresh and alive and crackling with warmth.

The pieces remain on the dining room table for a week or so. I finally sew together what is there and set the assemblage aside. ❁

Introduction

Not unlike other spiritual traditions, such as walking pilgrimage or silent meditation retreat, quiltmaking is a "way." It has the ability to become underlying structure for a patchwork life that informs all of one's work in the world. It can create context for experiencing all that one can be, moment by moment, stitch by stitch.

Every quilt has a story. I share life events through each telling. It's not a timeline, but rather a chronicle of hopes and dreams interchangeable with challenges and realizations in a nonlinear way. In a playground of many teachers and no one master, this book is my testimony to an infinitely rich weaving of consciousness with countless moments spent in sacred space, with Love.

Kathy Ford, 2017

Dream Reverie

In my dream I am aware that this is not a dream, this is real flesh and blood approaching, a large woman covered in a white, loose-fitting garment with long dark hair. She approaches me and looks deeply into my eyes. I recognize these eyes, my own eyes, my great grandmother's eyes, ancient eyes that glow from behind. I can see the edge of light where the eyeball meets the corner, and I am ecstatic, overwhelmed with wanting to touch and hug and feel and I am laughing and standing just inches from her, can't be close enough, and she is talking steadily, telling me a story that I know I am supposed to hear, but I am not listening. I don't hear or take in a word of what she is saying, just the unbroken rhythm of her voice uninterrupted by my joy, and my overwhelming desire to put my hands on her. I finally interrupt her to ask her name, and she pauses and says, Sun-night, and she smiles and continues with her story, now lying on her back looking up. I interrupt her again and beg her, please, just show me your wings, and while she continues talking, I see and feel the energy change and small wings, about half an arm's length, appear glimmering from underneath— they are not full grown yet—and then she is gone.

Kathy, 1962

1

Making Christmas

My little sewing machine was set up on the end of the dining room table. I was determined to make something that looked as good as the soft, red coat my mother had made for my doll. It was 1962 and I was four years old. I lifted my head. I could see her, standing at the kitchen stove through the open doorway, stirring something in a pot. I could be there right next to her if I wanted, standing on my stool to be tall enough for the task, helping to make her yummy macaroni and cheese. Or I could pull the stool over to the counter to stand next to her when she worked there. She would simply teach me how to do whatever she was doing, like rolling out the dough for our favorite Christmas sugar cookies, pushing the cookie cutter down into the thin dough, carefully getting it onto on the baking sheet without ruining the shape, and, the most fun of all, decorating with colored sugars. The visceral sensation of dragging that little one-step wooden stool around with me to ensure I could reach whatever surface I needed to, to be able to participate in whatever my mother was doing, is what stays with me today.

Dad was a fleeting presence back then, making a splash in the day when he arrived home. Like the time we heard a car honking in the driveway and looking out, saw Dad standing next to a brand new red convertible Mustang, beaming with joy. Or when he ceremoniously presented my mother with a brand new forty-five vinyl record of The Beatles hit song, *Twist & Shout,* and right there in their bedroom, pulled her out onto the floor to dance. I'm sure they didn't even see me standing there, barely three years old, holding onto the bedpost and swaying to the infectious beat. He was conveniently there when the scary monkeys in *The Wizard of Oz* appeared on the television set, sending me fly-ing into his arms for safety.

The early 1960s were a consistency of days with my mother wrapped around the space of creative innocence I was living in. It was a space of no time, just Mommy. She always smiles when she reminisces about those days, telling me that I was always there next to her, that she didn't think twice about including me in the task at hand. The image of her kneeling on the ground and making holes in the dirt for her flow-ers left an impression that would eventually bubble back up and grace my own gardens. Pansies were her favorites, like *little smiling faces,* she would say. When I had the chicken pox, she settled me on a daybed in the family room where she could see me from wherever she was. She actually let me watch *Superman* on the television. The sensation of being exactly where I was in that room still lives in me. She had given me a giant tootsie roll (still one of my favorites) in exchange for not scratching the itchy sores covering every inch of my body. One day I saw her crum-ple to the floor in a faint while standing at the stove stirring something. She told me to get help, and I had to run over to my neighbor all by myself. She was sick for a while after that, and I knew how to care for her just like she did for me.

One of my earliest memories was sitting in a big stuffed chair with little legs stretched out in front of me, a book of paper dolls in my lap, scissors in hand, imagining the feel of the tabs folding onto the waiting cardboard doll. But imagination had a life of its own, and my mind swung around to wondering what would happen if I cut that curious ridge off the new black pants Mommy had just bought me. I was as de-lighted with the hole that opened to show an oval of my skin below as I was with my paper dolls.

Imagination became the spark between me and my younger brother, too. As soon as he was old enough to sit at a table, Mom would serve us our favorite grilled cheese sandwiches and Campbell's bean-with-bacon soup at our very own child-sized table and chairs. My two-year-old brother would peer into the bowl and look up at me in wonder and say, *Look, little birdie eggs!* Even then, he could make me laugh.

My recollections of these few accessible moments have always been attached to where my mother was and what she was doing in relation to me and my brother. While I would instinctively go to my father's side of the bed in the middle of the night after a bad dream for comfort, it was always the tap tap tap of my mother at her typewriter each night that would spin the cocoon of safety for my imagination as I lay in the dark by myself.

Mother was the space of *no time* I had been carrying forward with me since the moment I was conceived. *Grandmother* was the space of *curiosity and wisdom* that began to open for me as a little girl.

I was the granddaughter of two very powerful women.

After arriving in this country at the age of twenty-one as a new bride, my Gramma Ford bore four children and devoted her life to nourishing her family. She never mastered English and never learned to drive, but she could control an entire household with just the smell of one of her Albanian pies, layers of her own homemade phyllo dough filled with an egg and onion mixture containing meat or spinach. My father tells the story of his own father calling home from the bar and grill he owned, summoning Dad most nights to bring him a plate of Gramma's supper. It wasn't that he didn't serve good Albanian food at his establishment—he did. It was the power of Gramma's cooking. It was all he wanted. I was six when my grandfather died, and Gramma lived for thirty more years alone, content and capable. Her way in the world was through the senses and expressing herself with her hands, and in her presence, it always felt as true and as important to me as any other way.

Gramma MacQueen was just forty-two when I was born, a glamorous businesswoman who loved to travel the world. I never knew my grandfather; he had died when my mother was sixteen. Gramma was always just Gramma, a force unto herself, living alone in each of the many homes she made for herself over the course of my childhood. She commanded attention by just walking through the door. She exuded a mixture of charm, will, and devotion to family. She always came bearing gifts, and at Christmas each one was wrapped as if the most precious jewel in the world. She started sharing her love of travel with me when I was four years old, taking me on my first train ride from Rochester to Buffalo. By the time I was eight, these simple excursions had led to annual trips each spring. At first, it was driving to major East Coast cities—Boston, New York, and Washington—visiting historic sites, family, and friends along the way. Eventually, she took me to Europe—to Paris, to the Alps for skiing, and to her apartment on the Costa del Sol in Spain.

While Gramma MacQueen filled her home with the beautifully crafted objects she would bring back from her exotic trips, Gramma Ford's home was a showcase for the many exquisite works of fabric, thread, and yarn that she had made herself. While Gramma Ford's well-used hands were soft and sturdy with naturally pink, clean nails, Gramma MacQueen's hands were modern, with painted red nails and fingers adorned with gold and jewels. Perhaps the polish was just a way for her to hide the dirt that would collect under her nails while digging in her beloved gardens. She never wore gloves, claiming that she needed to feel the earth directly on her hands.

I was six years old when we moved to our new home across town, conveniently within walking distance of the country club where we would spend languid summer days swimming and playing golf. During the winter, my brother and I would spend hours constructing igloo forts with our neighborhood friends in the many feet of snow that would fill the back yard. Together as a family, we would head to the indoor ice rink downtown to practice figure skating. And so life began to shift from the day-to-day of Mom's world to life out there in the bigger arena.

I loved being in the kitchen in the new house with the generous red Formica counters. I continued to practice cooking. I loved food, and developed an early talent for describing just how delicious something could be, with gusto, much to the amusement of my family. I received a copy of the children's Betty Crocker Cookbook and didn't waste any time making the Swedish meatballs and mashed potatoes, setting the dining room table, and serving the family dinner. At this point I had also graduated from my toy-sized sewing machine to Mom's pedal-driven Singer that lived in the guest room. I learned to make jumpers and skirts and culottes, and actually wore them too.

As Christmas approached, Mom would set up a series of folding tables in the basement and bring out boxes of beads, velvet ribbon, Styrofoam balls, and pins. We would sit together for hours making the most amazing ornaments for the Christmas tree, truly beautiful creations. We would invite our friends to come join in the fun. I couldn't wait to get down there each day and finish whatever I had started, Most were made to give as gifts. Making those ornaments held, for me, the essence of making Christmas.

Eventually, I began to make all my Christmas presents. It started with new stockings for Mom and Dad. The magic of Christmas morning seemed to be concentrated in the stockings each year; there, anticipation and joy could be stretched out over a longer period of time than it would take to rip into one large package. Our family stockings were uniquely decorated felt constructions that Mom had made. There was one for each of us with our name in bold felt letters at the top. For some reason, the only two that were stuffed full each year were for us kids. They were always ceremoniously propped outside our bedroom doors on Christmas morning, as if to say, *Santa gives you permission to have some joy right now without waiting for us* (i.e., we are exhausted from being up all night wrapping presents and need to sleep a little longer).

Mom and Dad's stockings remained downstairs, curiously almost empty.

The new stockings I made were also made of felt, twice as big, shaped like oversized elf boots and decorated with the lettering, *from your little elves.* Making Christmas for my parents became the thrill of finding things to wrap and put in these stockings each year. As co-conspirators in this exciting activity, my brother and I secretly went about making and acquiring all kinds of things to surprise our parents. We would walk to the big mall along the busy street near our house together, without supervision. Surprise was everything. I felt bubbly excitement at being able to turn the tables and make Christmas fun for my parents. Filling those stockings became a tradition that lasted for years, but it was just the beginning. From there, I went on to make shirts and nightgowns and elaborate bathrobes, even my first quilt, to offer in gratitude to my family, for the space I was being given to immerse myself in making things.

No one in my family was a quilter. Without a lineage or tradition to show me the way, I'm not sure what inspired me to make my first quilt. It was a simple pieced affair, squares of cotton polyester blends I picked out myself in the fabric section of Woolworths, quintessential sixties patterns and colors sewn in random combinations, backed with an olive green wide wale corduroy, and tied with embroidery floss. I was eleven years old. I loved making that quilt and giving it to my Gramma MacQueen for Christmas that year. She took it with her to every new house as she moved, and even at the end, it lived on her bed at the nursing home, covering her the morning she died.

The quilt felt like a success to me. It was an experience with beauty that could emerge from a seemingly random collection of pieces, and I wanted to do more. That led me to make a full-length patchwork maxi skirt for my mother. Lined, constructed with zipper, waistband, and a complementary sash to accentuate my mother's tiny waist, it was a unique

First quilt, 1969

combination of impulses, rudimentary skills, and determination. I don't think she wore it just to please me. I always had the sense that she really liked wearing the skirt, especially with the purple shirt she had found to go with it. But I didn't know for sure, and it didn't matter in the end. The reason for making things wasn't just the validation I would receive. It was the space of no time I could live in during the making.

During the spring of my junior year in high school, I found out that I hadn't been accepted to the summer program in France I had my heart set on. I sat in the library of my school with a pile of brochures and catalogs, crushed, determined to find another place to go. Anything to fill the gap that had been created by my disappointed expectation of a summer abroad. The six-week program in architecture at Carnegie Mellon University would do just fine, and with the support of my parents, I left for Pittsburgh without even knowing who Frank Lloyd

Wright was, let alone his famous house, Fallingwater, which I would be visiting during my time there. The program was structured in such a way as to introduce the rudiments of architectural design and practice. We even received an assignment to test our aptitude for structure. It was while working on this assignment—making a tower of a certain size with the least number of popsicle sticks—that I lost time. I sat down at my desk in the studio at ten o'clock in the morning, and when I asked what time it was after what had felt like only minutes, I was told it was four o'clock in the afternoon. After a rewarding summer of integrating this *no time* experience with the novelty of making architecture, I knew I had found my career path.

But still, every time I have been asked, *what is your heart's desire, the thing you would want to be doing 24/7 if you could?* my unequivocal response has always been, Making Christmas! For me, this meant creating context for magic. At Christmas, when all my day-to-day activities were motivated by a desire to make gifts of beauty and yummy things to eat, the child in me could fully engage in the process of making. Body memory would carry me along, as I worked late into the wee hours of Christmas morning, as I sewed on that last piece of trim or finished little wrapped packages for my parents' stockings. My heart's desire was to be swept up in a wave beyond my control without worrying about time, and then give the fruits of my labor away in anticipation of others' pleasure.

None of this has changed. Now, I find things all year long that I will buy or put aside, not knowing why or for whom, trusting that when it is time, I will know. As the unchallenged stocking queen of the family, this is my secret. The essence of making Christmas has come to mean following intuitive or emotional impulse to its natural conclusion. Rationality and purpose and intent may all enter and inform the process, but in the end, it comes down to trusting and believing in the truth that magic will always be there.

My creative spirit, which had been tapped as a child, was unleashed full force after the birth of my first child, Molly. I designed and made a quilt for my brother's wedding gift, wrote cookbooks, knitted my first sweater, and filled lined plastic crates, woven with colorful strips of fabric, with more homemade things. The following year I designed boxes, little architectural wonders with wood pieces cut in my carpenter neighbor's basement shop. They were stained and glued together with the help of my husband, and each one was filled with games for kids and adults alike. The checker/chess pieces for my parents were fashioned out of Sculpey clay, with a felt-backed checkerboard made of fabric. I collected little treasure toys for months for the kids, and crafted laminated word cards to complete the touch-and-tell games for their boxes. I was obsessed.

The next year, with baby Ben now in tow, in an attempt to resurrect the feeling of sitting at that basement ornament making table, I assembled all kinds of odd things: old Christmas cards, scraps of fabric, little wooden balls picked up at a novelty store, various strings and glitters and glue. I had absolutely no idea what I was going to make. It was just the barest impulse that started the process: thinking of a particular individual in my life, and while holding that energy, spontaneously fashioning an angel out of the various items strewn on the table. Each angel received a name and a story for the individual I had in mind. The quality of this particular effort would never be repeated, would never stretch through the years to produce the kind of familiarity that came with making "our" sugar cookies and "our" velvet beaded ornaments, or match the anticipation of stockings filled with lots of little wrapped things. But making Christmas had evolved and grown to include the feeling of spontaneity, and I liked it.

Every year some image comes into view that inspires me with its energy. Recently it was mittens. I had been in town gathering up the Christmas spirit and ideas for gifts. I saw a rack of mittens, clearly hand-crafted from what looked to be old sweaters. *I can do this!* The seed of a challenge planted, I spent the next week letting it germinate. I went through my drawers first to consider what sweaters I was done with, anything with holes or worn thin. I was enamored with the idea of making something sustainable and special and practical. I wondered about a pattern, what the process would be, and finally turned to the internet. There was a wealth of information and many references to a pattern that had apparently been around forever. I experimented with it to get a variety of sizes. I had polar fleece scraps that could be used for lining. I had to determine a method for fitting and sewing all the pieces together, like a puzzle. It became clear very quickly not only that I was engaged in a fast and easy method for making beautiful mittens, but that the creative combinations and variations on this theme were endless. The image grew into a simple, warm, soft, and pliable mitten for

Christmas mittens

both men and women alike, something to reach for on the coldest of winter days. I made many visits to the local hospice thrift store and ended up with a small stockpile of cheap used wool sweaters of varying knits and designs. I added to this an old knit wool jacket that I had lovingly worn for at least twenty years, and which was now riddled with too many visible holes. I put them all through hot wash and dry cycles to felt the wool. I cut everything up into usable pieces. My entire sewing area, typically dedicated to quilting, was devoted to this endeavor and within a week, I had made ten pairs of gorgeous mittens.

It all happened very quickly. The simplicity of each mitten felt good. I found myself thinking of ways I could embellish or add stitching—in effect, making them more complicated and taking more time. I had to keep reminding myself that it was okay for something so wonderful to be so easy and to feel so good. I finally realized that the gift of making these mittens was in the joy *and* the restraint, in the economy and the richness. Each pair had a person attached to it, an energy that I had been feeling and connecting with during the process of making. I felt the certain symmetry of my hands making something for the hands of a loved one, an energetic heart-to-heart connection through design with color, texture, softness, and warmth. The spirit of making Christmas, with its history and heartbeat, continued to firmly hold my love of making things in place.

It would be over twenty years after making my grandmother's quilt before I made another. ❄

Reverie

I just finished piecing the quilt top with my beloved twenty-year-old Singer sewing machine the night before. The machine is resting against the wall. We had to move the table to make room to lay everything out. Legs stretched out to allow my body to engage fully, I am one with this quilt on the floor of my parent's dining room. It is a hot summer morning. I woke at dawn, and began working right away, basting the finished top to batting and backing, at the same time contemplating options for the hand-quilted lines that would stitch it all together. The baby's things are placed close by so I can still be with her in the hours it will take for me to complete this first task. Three months of design and construction after ten years of its presence living in me. A lifetime of saving fabric scraps for something special. Each band of the rich blue and yellow gold frames a precious jewel. I am fascinated with the order that emerges even from a crazy-quilt-inspired approach to construction. It will take another year to complete the hand quilting I am now teaching myself, with the aspiration to gift this quilt to my beloved brother and his new bride.

My breasts are full of milk for my new baby. When she is in my arms, I can give over control completely to her need. She'll be awake soon and, temporarily, I will have to leave the work of yielding to the need of this quilt that wants resolution.

Kathy with Quilt # 1, 1991

2

Discovering Order

I was sitting in my college library on an unusually sparkling winter day, senior year in early 1980. As an honors student, I had been assigned a desk for the year in the bowels of the third floor, a place to keep all my research in a lockable cage where I could work quietly and privately. But I couldn't bear being in the dark that day. By contrast, the library's public quiet room was a mezzanine that faced east and looked out through large panes of unobstructed glass onto one of the many historic greens of the campus. I was lucky enough to find an unoccupied place there. Settled in and sitting comfortably in one of the large overstuffed chairs, I was finally beginning to work in earnest on my thesis. I was feeling quite sure of myself—filled with hubris, actually—imagining that I was doing something important and groundbreaking. The plan was to draw the ideal city of Sforzinda, a theoretical Renaissance city that, to date, had only been described in words in a four-hundred-year-old treatise. The path to this starting point had already been a long one, involving copious investigations into the Renaissance obsession with mathematics and architectural order, searching for and finding obscure references to this particular ideal city that I could actually understand, and finally, convincing the college to procure a copy of the out-of-print English translation of the treatise for my use. Now, with the oversized red volume prominently open in my lap, I began to read the first paragraph. Three hours later I was still reading this first paragraph. Not only was I at a loss as to how words on the page would translate into architectural form, I was experiencing an odd sensation of getting sucked into the space between the words. Confidence that I was in control of this process dissolved. I finally realized there were multiple, maybe even infinite, ways for me to interpret this paragraph graphically. I could spend the entire semester just documenting all the possible variations. Furthermore, the three-dimensional sketches of individual buildings offered in the margins of the text looked like they were from another planet, like Gaudí sculpture, twisting curved spires and flowing molded surfaces that bore no relation to the strict order that was implied in the plans. With a sinking feeling that bordered on panic, I realized that I didn't have enough time in the space of just one semester to do what I had proposed to do.

That was the end of the proposed thesis. I began to consider the strange images drawn in the margins of the treatise's text, and the thesis was recrafted to become, instead, an exploration of form in relation to language—how the space of interpretation that exists between the two creates a context for something both known and unexpected to emerge.

I was supported by an advisor who, as a onetime monk, now professor of philosophy, would sit with me in his office, in silence, while I smoked a cigarette, encouraging me to wait patiently for the next intuitive moment to present itself and be communicated. The week before the final written thesis was due, I sequestered myself in the historic house that now contained the art department. It was a ten-minute walk from campus, just far enough away for me to create the context of isolation I thought I needed. I was desperate. I felt the truth of my vision that something was there in this work, but also felt the stress of not having enough time to see it and bring it to light. For two days and nights I never left the grand living room of this house. I paced. Sat at the large work table for as long as I could take it, papers spread around me, searching for the thread that would bind all of the pieces that had been documented so far. Slept on the couch. Smoked more cigarettes. Forced myself to stay there until some form of resolution came.

I did end up writing something and putting it into the hands of my housemate back on campus who was typing the final copy for me. But

I knew that I had raced time and lost. I could feel truth there in the gaps between the words and images even if I didn't fully grasp the structure of it yet. The final paper that emerged from my work that semester was dense with referenced research and extensive footnotes, episodic in character, and by no means proved anything. But what I learned and proved to myself was that the patterns of all things, both verbal and visual, are mutually dependent upon one another. I learned that meaning, whether expressed in words or images, could come from the same source. It was the stuff of relationship, and I couldn't just think myself through. It felt like failure even though my advisor and the two outside readers who attended my review offered highest honors, congratulations, and encouragement to continue with the exploration. Was I willing to sacrifice success for this effort? I continued to be drawn to that gap between seeing and feeling like the proverbial moth to the flame, but it was no longer as an academic chasing an abstract concept. Now it was as a young woman chasing passion—and also a desire for safety. Choosing architecture school felt like a more predictable course. This undergraduate work was just preparation, after all, for becoming the very best architect I could be.

I went to New York to work for a year while applying to graduate schools. I like to say that I started becoming a quiltmaker that year. I share this story with my oldest and dearest friend Kathy. We met when we were ten years old, survived her family moving to a different state when we were thirteen, and went through college years with little contact, only to find ourselves reunited and living together in New York City upon our respective graduations. We had no idea at the time that many years later, we would be engaged in parallel worlds of quiltmaking.

One year living together in the tiny apartment on East 81st in NYC in 1981 made us the independent and completely connected beings that we still are today. With the only light coming in through one small, heavily gated window and door out to a tiny back cement courtyard, there was a quality of living in the womb with a twin. We shared every-thing—even the same name—in darkened space that cocooned the yearnings of two twenty-two-year-old women. It was a riotous year rid-ing a roller coaster of emotion that included jealously, joy, hurt, and compromise.

One winter morning we were walking to work along First Avenue to-gether, arguing about something. I can't remember which one of us actu-ally crossed over to the other side of the street in fury to continue plodding along. First Avenue is a wide street, and even with that large gap, complete with moving cars and dirty mounds of snow lining the street separating us, we continued yelling at each other. It was empowering to feel the force of my anger truly met in that broad space. We both finally burst out laughing at the same time. I can still feel the gut-level relief after all this time, and the healing that came with the laughter.

I was working as an intern in an architecture firm while applying to graduate programs, and I was fascinated with crazy quilts. There was something about the immediacy of sewing one piece of fabric to another without any pre-conceived notion of what the result would be that felt true for me. And whereas I appreciated the fine embroidery and lush materials used in the Victorian-era pieces crafted by women of leisure, it was the random practice of piecing odd bits of cloth together as a money-saving habit leftover from Colonial times that seemed to speak most directly to me.

I was sitting at my drafting table on a rainy Saturday afternoon in the little room that was my bedroom off the kitchen, feeling the urge to randomly piece odd bits of fabric together like a crazy quilt. But I didn't have any fabric and thread. Instead, I used the drafting tools of my trade and followed a few simple, arbitrarily chosen rules to draw six blocks of twenty pieces each onto square pieces of paper. Not only was there no logic to the placement of the shapes in each block drawing, I had no preconception about what to do with them or how they would be put together. I was getting further and further lost in my thoughts, not completely aware that the abstractness of this endeavor, drawing lines on paper, was leading me away from the actual experience of making something as visceral and tactile as a crazy quilt. Kathy was standing on the other side of the open doorway looking at me with a mixture of disbelief and impatience. When she asked what I was doing, I said, "I'm making a pattern for a crazy quilt," not realizing that I had just uttered an oxymoron. She hesitated for only a moment, until she realized that I might actually choose to stay there drawing rather than go out and play with her. Then she said, "Put your pencil down. We're going out!"

The heartbreak I felt on the eve of her departure for Australia with her Australian husband ten years later went deep. By then I had been to graduate school and back, had gotten married, and had started my career in architecture while she blossomed in marketing. Our social circles were just beginning to blend. I couldn't believe she was leaving. We would be entering this next exciting phase of life, of making our own families, with half the earth separating us.

The year after she moved, as I was preparing to give birth to my first child, I unearthed the block tracings I had saved from that first brush with making a crazy quilt. Now, with crinkly, yellowing pieces of paper and faded pencil lines, I had the idea that I would make a quilt to give to my brother and his fiancée for a wedding present. I was now living in what had once been my husband's artist studio. It was a glorious home filled with continuous north light from the huge double-hung windows that lined the entire space. The loft was essentially one open room with fifteen-foot ceilings and sliding Japanese-style partitions to create the most minimal separation. The only actual door in the loft at this point was to the tiny room we created for baby Molly. Setting up the sewing machine was a challenge, and I settled for the small table that backed up to the one couch in the room. It was smack-dab in the center of life in the loft and though I had to put everything away at the end of any work session, the openness and light in this centered place gave me the support I needed to begin spreading my wings as a quiltmaker.

And so the process began. To honor the crazy quilt tradition, I chose twenty fabrics from a variety of sources. I had boxes full of scraps from from making my own clothes as a teenager, bottoms of cut-off pants, the remains of favorite old things, and lots of unused vintage yardage. To this stock I added some new pieces and made selections entirely by intuition. I stacked up the fabric in two piles of ten layers each, used each of the six block tracings as patterns, and cut out stacks of shapes. I wanted a rule, even if arbitrary, that could guide me in sewing each block together without actually planning it. In this case, I simply arranged the stacks so that I could make forty blocks without a single repeat of fabric in any one shape.

For some reason, the fact that there would be no two shapes of the same fabric anywhere in the quilt felt thrilling. Even so, there would still be some implicit order in the repeating shapes in each of the six blocks. Would this be visible? What would be the overall effect? With the spontaneous pairing of fabrics, uncertainty consistently yielded to pleasure. Each block was different, reminiscent of the uniqueness of a stained glass window. And yet they all felt the same too, much like the

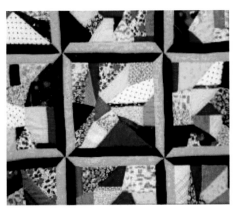

Quilt #1, detail

feeling of viewing a group of stained glass windows from afar. I don't think I was completely conscious at the time that making frames for each of these blocks with the sashing (strips of fabric sewn around or between blocks of a quilt top) was, in effect, framing each pane of glass. When the top was completed, I realized that what I had made was an *ordered crazy quilt*. I finished the top in time to present it as the wedding gift for my brother, and then spent a year hand quilting it with simple lines that outlined each shape of fabric— just in time to present it as a first-anniversary gift.

Inspired and curious to explore this process further, I began a second quilt. I made tracings for four new blocks of sixteen pieces each, not quite as random, a bit more ordered to a square. I chose sixteen fabrics, made my stacks of cut shapes and completed twenty-four blocks in the same manner without any preconceived notion of how they would be structured within a quilt. When they were finished, the most dominant characteristic I saw was a prominence of yellow in contrast to the rest of the fabrics. Diagonals appeared between the contrasting pieces and prompted me to rotate the blocks. Turning the twenty-four blocks on a forty-five-

Quilt #2, 1993

degree angle created an equal number of "empty spaces" in between and the need for an order that would visually balance and tie together at the same time.

Awareness of the relationship between the individual blocks and the spaces between them was familiar. As an architecture student, I had been infinitely interested in the tension between what could be planned and what could be seen or discovered as a basis for design. Most of my design efforts were frustrated by my inability to reconcile this interest with the function or program that I was designing for. As a quiltmaker however, having a process within which to experience those moments was like magic. With a leap of faith, I could begin a process with the presupposition that the order was *there,* that I would just have to be open to see it, and that I eventually would see it. I didn't have to plan it in advance. And I could acknowledge its importance by making beautiful connections with pieces of fabric as I saw them. I finished a second quilt with the confidence that I could find order in any disparate, crazily assembled group of elements. Now I could give it a name: I was discovering order.

While working on the hand quilting for Quilt #2, I began a third quilt in this series, which was pieced and basted as I was preparing to give birth to my second child. I believe the subsequent birth of my son Ben, born with Down Syndrome, played no small part in the continuing development of my ideas about and fascination with discovering order. In one shattering moment, I learned that I had absolutely no control at all over an outcome. Work on Quilt #3 halted. It would be seven years before I finished it.

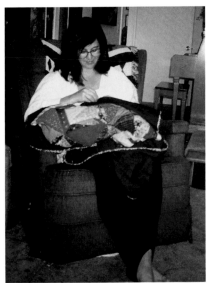

Kathy with Quilt #2, 1993

A gap developed in the trajectory of my progress as a quiltmaker in the years following Ben's birth. I sometimes wonder about this gap and what it made space for. What did I need to learn or experience to allow me to move forward as an artist? My work as an architect had developed my ability to negotiate many diverse needs and create structure, in the form of roadmaps that could allow for client participation, change, and adaptation all the way through construction in a positive way. But this was very different from my orthodox professional training, which placed ultimate value on a finalized plan and its associated details even before construction began. I liked tradition. It felt important to preserve the feel of something known in the process of creating something new. But I was learning that in renovation, when you begin to open up walls and discover what is really there, you can never fully control the outcome. Uncontrolled outcomes always cost extra time and money. The patterns of my quiltmaking evoked tradition and mystery that felt equally true to me. But these two endeavors that organized my artistic impulses were still not connected in my mind. How could I reconcile time and money with lack of control? It was as if I were skiing down a gentle slope with each ski in its own groove in the snow, with no way to spontaneously turn in any other direction without falling.

The last quilt in this series represented the final transition from life in NYC to a new home in Amherst, MA. I moved to a little rented house with the kids while my husband continued to commute back to the loft in New York. There was very little room for anything other than beds and some simple furniture in this transitional home. I found an old vanity

Quilt #4, progress detail

table at a flea market and set my sewing machine on top of it in the bedroom. Sewing there was like an afterthought, a place to occupy just barely on the only section of open wall between the window and bathroom door. I sat there with the stacks of shapes for the next quilt piled up on the meager leftover edge of the table, full of anticipation for working with the rich shades of blue and red and gold. The centered form of a sparkling star that emerged in each block was clearly and enticingly apparent even in the serendipity of fabric choices.

When it was time to put them all together, I was drawn to mark a literal center in this quilt while at the same time making sure it wouldn't be completely obvious. The impulse was to honor this center as something visibly connected and integrated with the texture of the rest of the quilt, but not make it stand out too loudly. It felt more like an invitation. After years of being tossed about in the craziness of juggling marriage, motherhood, and career, of honoring the needs of husband, children, and business colleagues, a yearning to sit in this eye of the storm became visible. Being there in that balanced centered place required a kind of exposure my calculating, rationally trained mind could only understand in abstract. Staying open to the possibility of seeing something new and exciting and beautiful became a way in. I could be aware and not have to understand. Quiltmaking was becoming my most direct process for seeing patterns and experiencing light-filled moments in a clear way, even if meaning remained elusive.

Discovering order had followed me, after that first awakening in college, through architecture school, into my career as an architect, into marriage and divorce, my child-rearing years, through years of yoga and varied forms of embodied movement, through energy medicine training, and most significantly, into the heart of every artistic endeavor I explored. These two simple words could open up the bottomless well of creativity I saw in front of me every day.

They are the two words that continue to describe a sacred place of *no time* in which I find myself when engaged in the process of making something. ❁

Quilt #4, 2001

Reverie

I am napping and, having just fallen into the space between waking and dreaming, I hear a voice say very clearly, two doors will close, two doors will open. My heart is pounding.

What does this mean?

Quilt #3, detail

3

Two Doors

I spent my junior year of college in New York City studying at an Institute for Architecture and Urban Studies. The brainchild of architect Peter Eisenman, the Institute offered the equivalent of a year abroad for aspiring architects from small liberal arts colleges. Located on the top floor of a building on West 41st Street directly across from the New York Public Library, it felt like we were in the center of the universe. Gathered in the gallery for our first lesson from program director Eisenman, we listened to a short speech that highlighted our privileged status as academics with the resources and ability to study liberal arts and become intellectuals. He noted that we were all accomplished already and confident in our endeavors. He made sure we understood the expanse of thought we took for granted in relation to the limited expanse of our life experience. He finished with a clear and frightening proposition, telling us that by the end of our year there, we would all be questioning *everything*. No idea, thought, or design would be exempt from the rigor of questioning. We would learn to operate in a space where absolutely nothing could be taken for granted.

One of our first assignments was to examine the nature of the design process by transforming a door into a space of transition. We were given a set of rules for transforming the material elements that defined the door: the wall surrounding and supporting the opening, the frame, any relevant ornament, the door itself, and so on. I dove in and quickly finished the exercise, only to hear from my teacher the next day that I had done it incorrectly. I hadn't embraced the intent of the exercise, namely, to explore the limits of human scale or imbued cultural meaning in a way that respected the design elements of this particular door assembly.

I had a hard time accepting that I had personalized the process and changed the very character of each element by arbitrarily altering form in a way that made it unrecognizable. Asked to repeat the assignment by "following the rules," this time, I resisted. After all, I was the artist, the one in control. I was the one creating the meaning, right?

Following the rules the second time around actually turned out to be liberating. I realized that the rules had no inherent meaning in themselves. The meaning that emerged through this exercise could only come from the cultural meaning that each element of the original door carried, the strength of a column defined by its proportions, the sculptural beauty of trim ornament defined by how it caught the light, the load bearing capability of a lintel defined by its shape, the level of transparency possible in the plane of the door itself defined by the very material it was made of. It wasn't about designing for a specific program or function. So what guided the design? The process seemed arbitrary, but in hindsight, I know that for me, it was clearly guided by intuition. I couldn't have predicted or planned the next decision or operation because without a program, there was no reason to. Nor was there any way to know how the experience of the design would change with each step of the process. It was my first conscious experience of how the impulse to move in a certain direction, in a certain way, could be supported by structure that I was in relation to, but not necessarily in control of.

In this exercise, intuition reared up to make its presence known at a time in my life when intellect had been leading the charge of all my pursuits. I was an avid reader of Ayn Rand and I'm pretty sure I had read *Atlas Shrugged* at least twice by then. I thought it was a brilliantly constructed novel, captivating in its complex layering of story and philosophy. Even her one-dimensional characters, either champions of intellect *or* champions of feeling, lived in a world that seemed possible to me at the time. Her heroes were the champions of the intellect, Aristotle, and capitalism. The heroine was a successful businesswoman, as was my smart grandmother. Unlike the heroine however, who was an heiress who never had children, Gramma MacQueen was self-made, one of the first women in this country to sell commercial real estate. She built her company from determination and hard work, often at the expense of her only child, my mother. There was no middle ground or gray area for a mother's intuition to co-exist with business in Ayn Rand's world, and I suspect there wasn't for Gramma either. It was easy to embrace the world of the intellect that was being modeled for me and ignore the brush with intuition I had just experienced.

But later on in the year at the Institute, it happened again. This time in a history class, where we were being asked to present an analysis of geometric relationships and spatial congruences in the design of a Renaissance villa from Palladio's *Four Books of Architecture*. When I presented my model, the look on my professor's face told me that the undulating, translucent blue plastic that I used to describe flow of space through the rooms of the villa was too much of a departure from what was expected. I had translated a *sense* of something into form, literally. He wanted to see the logic of the form, abstractly translated in a Renaissance way. Intellect had failed me. Even so, I was congratulated for taking a risk. This was the same professor who later wrote on one of my evaluations, *Kathy continues to belie her rather personable manner in her ability to handle difficult work.*

I arrived in graduate school with the expectation that I could continue to take risks. But this was professional school, and it didn't take more than a semester to realize I had to perform a certain way or I would fail. I almost quit, but I was just passionate enough, still, about being an architect that I stayed the course. By the time I got to my final thesis I was confident enough to look intuition directly in the eye. I wanted to find a way to infuse the process of design with the mysterious and unknown. My simple housing project proposal would take advantage of an urban historic context that included a waterfall and abandoned factory buildings. I loved drawing random sections through the site in an effort to capture inspired hints of what was there, existing structures in relation to energies, unseen but felt, in the topography and history of this place. I designed the project from these sections first, and the plans followed (function following form). In this, I was challenging the orthodoxy of my training (form following function). My process, one that I believed had opened a door for intuitive design decisions, did produce credible enough housing. But my search for liberation had failed. I was repeatedly asked the question, *Why did you do it this way?* and I didn't have a clear answer. I was acknowledged for taking a risk by one professor, chastised for departing from the orthodoxy of our training by another. As a colleague offered after my final review, *your politics and your architecture just aren't aligned.*

By the time I had finished the first two quilts in the years following Molly's birth, I could confidently incorporate a spontaneous, intuitive gesture into the design. I had begun the process again with the third quilt. The blocks were quite large this time, sixteen squares of sixteen squares, made of pieces of various solid colors, some with an edge of printed fabric sliced in at a random diagonal. Enjoying the episodic quality that resulted (once again) from sewing pieces together without a plan, I wasn't prepared for the disappointing experience of seeing the finished blocks assembled. The whole was not very interesting, more like background instead of the centerpiece around which one would traditionally make a frame with sashing. I couldn't find anything distinctive to highlight or celebrate. I decided to put it aside for a while.

As I entered more fully into motherhood, it was clear to me that my two design paths, making architecture and making quilts, were not speaking to each other. My professional life as an architect was the door I opened when I needed validation for being responsible, for being a supportive partner and family member, and most importantly, for being a smart, independent woman who was successful in her work. My creative life as a quiltmaker was the door I opened when I needed to connect with mystery and spirit, where I could honor intuition. What was in the space in between? I didn't know because I had come to believe I couldn't walk through the door and claim my life as a creative person unless I closed the door to my life as a professional first. *Was this the meaning of the two doors in the dream?*

When I became pregnant again, my relationship to my career as an architect had shifted. I no longer worked for a firm, and I was filling the space between jobs with teaching architecture at an area college. Molly was two years old and just starting preschool. I'd seen the sonogram with the baby in the womb at three months, when bleeding started. An energetic and vibrant force even then, I saw the perfect spine and kicking legs and believed that this baby was not only healthy, but absolutely meant to be. The problem seemed to be the placenta that covered my cervix; I was ordered to bed rest for the middle three months of my pregnancy.

We made up the convertible sofa bed in the middle of the living room, which could allow me to be the center of all activity. Determined to be productive in the enforced stillness of so many hours each day, I decided to teach myself how to hand piece a quilt. I'd saved an image of a design that brought to life for me a play of circles within a traditionally pieced set of blocks. There was no accompanying pattern, but because it was a symmetrical design, I only had to figure out one section. Intrigued, I sketched a diagram for how blocks could be put together to achieve a similar result. My husband brought me pieces of cardboard, pencil, paper, and an X-Acto knife, all things I was skilled with from making architectural models, and right there in my lap, I fashioned a crude set of templates to use as guides for cutting out fabric and making seam lines. I had a beautiful cut of turquoise print fabric that would probably be enough for the main body of the design, and lots of scraps to work the rest of the pieces. I had to make all the fabric choices for the entire quilt before I could even begin to sew if I wanted to be sure the design would work. I enjoyed the challenge of making everything fit. All I needed was some thread, a needle, and a pair of scissors to start.

Hand piecing, 1993

It was exciting at first. I loved the accomplished feeling of making the small, even stitches that comprised each seam, just like in the days before sewing machines. I loved how I could control exactly where the needle would go to create very precise points at corners where acute angles met. I loved the feeling of being so intimately connected to what I was making. I was practicing an intuitive hand-to-heart connection that felt good. But as satisfying as the precision of this method was, of being able to control the outcome, it didn't take long for me to get bored and restless. The whole process began to feel tedious. Once everything was figured out, there was no place for my imagination to go, nothing for my intellect to engage with that felt worthy. The project was abandoned as soon as I came off bed rest.

My Gramma Ford had made intricate cutwork, crochet lace, and weavings as a young woman in Albania. *Women's work.* I was in awe of the skill and patience required to fill a trunk with the decorative household linens that covered furniture throughout her home. The big tablecloths must have taken forever, repeating the same patterns over and over to achieve a finished product as impressive to me as an intricately detailed building facade. She still had a drawer full of finely crocheted lace yokes that had never been made into garments. And then there was the red patterned blanket that lay on the floor in her living room. It was rug thick, tightly woven with a bold pattern that included deep golds and blues. I imagined the passion and intellect of my quiet grandmother living forever in these skillfully made treasures. Did I have the persistence and patience to master my version of women's work in a similar way? Or was my intellect demanding a different way to relate to quiltmaking?

I had a dream early during the pregnancy in which the baby presented himself and told me his name was Ben, and we called him Ben from that moment on. Coming off bed rest after my sixth month, Ben remained happily in the womb to full term, and helped support the belief that all was well. The time spent hand piecing now became the way to settle myself in the gaps between the bigger activities of the day.

Belief is powerful energy! I simply believed I was going to have a perfect baby. But when it was time to deliver, he couldn't get out on his own. After days of the attending midwife's patient ministrations, the decision was made to do an emergency C-section, and I was given local anesthesia. I'll never forget the way Ben stared into my soul just moments after he was wrapped in a blanket and placed in his father's arms at birth. All the doubt I had experienced while watching his limp, flaccid body being pulled out of my womb disappeared.

The nurses had been tiptoeing around me and evading my questions as I was moved from recovery to a private room. I demanded that my baby be brought in to me when I woke up a few hours later. Alone with Ben for the first time since his birth, I looked down into his beautiful face and registered the pure love I was feeling. Pediatrician Joe, famous for his *after noon only* hospital visits, sailed into the room at eight o'clock that morning. With fanfare and cheerfulness, he whisked Ben out for his exam and upon return, in the same cheerful voice simply said, "Well, he's healthy as a horse. But there's a problem. He has Down syndrome." The shock of the news elicited a wail of grief with such force as to lift me off the bed. And then it was over. From that moment on, all the spaces in my life that had served as the connective tissue supporting all that I am simply become something different. I was the mother of a perfect baby boy with Down syndrome. Like the relief of a sweet cool breeze flowing through a room on a hot day, I experienced how belief can simply change in an instant.

Shortly after Ben's birth, I was drawn to finish piecing Quilt #3. I started thinking about how thinner spaces of sashing could take on the quality of a centerpiece instead of the blocks themselves. What kind of pattern or figure could complement the character of the diagonal created in the clipped squares of each block? How many layers of order could be built in? Would this reversal of "special" and "normal" be apparent? What emerged was the establishment of five centers, four of which framed and anchored two portals and a star. Overall balance was reinforced by introducing a repeating blue square, the use of the color black, and a quilting stitch design to complete the quilt with varying densities of gridded lines. Riding the surge of energy following Ben's birth, I was able to finish sewing the quilt top together within a few weeks.

The challenges of daily life in New York City with two young children, finding services for Ben's special needs, and worrying about the path of my career, all competed for priority. My time for quilting continued to occupy the very narrow spaces of free time in my life, not unlike the narrow spaces of sashing in this quilt. I was actively seeking out and engaging in new spiritual practices that included dream journaling, yoga retreats, and all aspects of holistic health that focused on nourishment. I even went through a brief period during which I considered becoming a doctor, to create a professional context for working with the energy medicine that consistently called to me. Eventually, the pull of these practices led me to the realization that it was time to leave New York. In 1998, an opportunity for architecture partnership presented itself in Massachusetts and I took it.

I finally picked up Quilt #3 again during the year of settling with the kids in our new home in Amherst while my husband commuted back to NYC during the week. The first year in our rented house was marked by hours of steadily hand quilting the gridded lines that helped to both anchor and accentuate. Anchor us in our new life. Accentuate where change was taking place and where patience was called for to negotiate a long-distance marriage that was struggling. Ben's birth had signaled a moment of truth for me and his father. I had retreated to my coping mechanism of overdrive, and he had retreated to an unreachable place. Years of therapy would not yield a clear commitment from either one of us to find a new way to communicate. Meanwhile, I was learning how support precedes action through my yoga practice. I had found a path for my vulnerable heart to express itself, to feel supported in the flow of color and form and texture that I could see, and to feel intimately with my hands at the same time. I needed the support of the intuition that lived in my quiltmaking to inform the rest of my life. I was beginning to see a pattern. I was learning to open the door in my head and watch for where another opened to real life through my heart. Two doors in tandem working together.

Quilt #3 was finally finished in 1999 as we moved from the rental into a historic house that would be our home for the next fifteen years. The quilt lived on our bed, a witness to the struggle to keep our marriage alive. There was a small room with a window that could only be accessed through our bedroom, used as a closet by the previous owners. At first, this room was simply a rug on the floor where I did my yoga practice. It quickly morphed into a quilting studio where I would commune with my creative spirit during quiltmaking, away from the bustle of the rest of the house. For the next ten years, this room was the place time would stop for me, and it became my refuge from the pain of separation and divorce from my husband.

Before

I eventually relocated the studio and began the process of fully restoring this room with a new man in my life. He did a beautiful job replastering all the walls and putting in a new sheetrock ceiling. But he had never really committed to finishing it himself, and we never found a way to finish it together. This once-sacred room in my home was now completely empty, painting still unfinished, and the door always closed. When he and I finally parted, I opened the door to this room, knowing that I would get to it when I was ready. A few months later, I walked in and decided that the new pale yellow walls with primed white trim were just fine the way they were. As it was, the room reminded me that even without perfection, there was beauty and light and growth and hope. After the hurt and

After

heartache of yet another parting with a man I loved, I was now finally letting myself accept pain. I put the thick blanket/rug my Albanian grandmother carried in her arms to America when she was twenty-one years old on the floor and on the wall in front of it, hung the quilt that I had started when I was pregnant with Ben, the one that took nearly seven years to finish. Quilt #3 had become the focus that created context for meditation. In its presence I could settle and observe the relationship between me and the universe, every day. ❀

Quilt #3, 2000

Dream Reverie

I am walking into a cage with a lion and its trainer. I have my back to the lion and it charges me, roaring, but I don't flinch or scream, just stand there with full confidence that the trainer will keep the lion from harming me. The lion then starts licking me, putting his head under my arm and hand, and I pet his head. The lion lies down next to me and I openly stroke his back. He starts rubbing me, nudging his head up my shirt in the back and re-emerges in the front as a little boy who hugs me close. I gently pull the little boy out from underneath my shirt. He walks away toward the cage and I see him transform back into the lion.

Energy Garden, 2002

4

Energy Garden

When we bought the big red house in Amherst, there was no garden to speak of, only the gorgeous white peonies we were told would arrive in June, located at the edge of a lawn along the dirt road leading to the house. I wasn't thinking garden at first. It took some time to settle into the awe I felt the moment I stepped into this historic place. The owner had just died and her son placed the house on the market almost immediately. I was the first to see it. There had been no staging or preparing the house for view. I walked through room after room cluttered with the debris left by an elderly woman who had been ill and bedridden for years. A lifetime of stuff was in the process of being moved into large black plastic bags scattered everywhere. It didn't matter. The spirit of the house was strong enough to propel me excitedly through each room. I moved up the narrow, winding back stair behind my real estate agent with a conviction that this would soon be home. We hadn't even seen the upstairs rooms yet when I said, "We need to make a full price offer right now, don't we?" My husband was in New York and had only seen the house from the outside. When I called, he simply said, "Just get it."

Even though this house sat on an equally spirited piece of land, my focus and attention went to settling inside first. There were so many rooms to fill in this 1850s gem. Neighborhood lore held that it had been a tavern stop on the Pony Express route between Boston and Albany in its day. That would explain the large room that occupied one half of the original footprint of the house, complete with three-flue brick fireplace. This room was filled up like an attic with things that didn't want to be seen, while exposed knob-and-tube wiring peeked out from crumbling plaster walls and ceiling. It had been a family home for the past fifty-five years. I learned from my neighbor that even with children grown and gone, the retired couple moved into their golden years as real Yankee homesteaders here. They did everything themselves, including growing more food than they could eat in a large vegetable garden that was now just an energetic imprint in the established expanse of lawn outside.

My motivation to make a garden was strong. After only two summers of hands in the dirt, taming a small yard at our bungalow in the Catskills, I was hooked on this simple and powerful way of connecting with Mother Earth. We had bought into a summer co-op colony located on top of a small mountain in the Borscht Belt of New York State the year before moving to Massachusetts. It was a haven from the overwhelming amount of concrete, noise, and smell that we were living with. From NYC, I could get there with the kids in just an hour and a half on a weekday with no traffic, and I couldn't wait to make the dramatic transition from *intensely urban* to *intensely country* each week. The summer of 1997 was our first, and we were able to juggle our schedules so that the kids could be there for five continuous weeks. It was like summer cohousing: Picnic tables outside inviting neighbors to eat and share time. Kids roaming and playing freely within the giant oval greens around which our little fifty-year-old bungalows were arranged. With constant attention and determination, my garden there blossomed. Now, it was easy to imagine collaborating with a piece of earth here in our new home in Amherst, too.

It wasn't that I was such a great gardener. Gardening was never even a passing thought in all my years of living in New York City. But I had managed to turn a wildness of invasive vines into something ordered, colorful and fragrant. I knew gardens like this required vigilant maintenance if you wanted them to keep evolving. The master gardeners I knew possessed this kind of commitment. But I still regarded a growing season like a project that might have a final completion date. I was just learning about the wonder of perennials and their role in a developing relationship with annuals.

I began digging up the lawn at our new home in Amherst within months of moving in. That was the summer of 1999. By the following spring, I was able to plant a handful of perennials—irises, daylilies, daisies, and hostas—to supplement the gorgeous peonies that already lived there. After three years of incrementally enlarging the ratio of dirt to grass, my new garden was finally showing signs of adolescent maturity. It was now the summer of 2002, the summer I signed up for my first year of "Quilting by the Lake" (QBL), a well-established quilting conference in western New York State. I would be participating in a week-long workshop, learning new techniques for making images of nature with fabric and thread. In preparation, I spent days in my young garden snapping photos, trying to capture the essence of the potency I was feeling, finally printing and packing these images, symbolic seeds and starts, inside a suitcase full of the fabric that would coax them into life.

While in graduate school, I had travelled for a summer with a Eurail pass through Europe to see architecture, to have memorable experiences, and to negotiate a path for myself as a twenty-five-year-old independent woman. The final destination before returning to London for the flight home was my grandmother's apartment on the Costa del Sol in Spain. On my way there, I visited the Alhambra in Granada, a masterpiece of Moorish architecture that held me captive for an entire morning. It was while I was sitting in one of the open arched windows, gazing into one of the many magnificent gardens there, that Philippe found me. It didn't take long to fall into a dynamic of sharing experiences with this man, expressing my passion for architecture. He was a self-proclaimed bull-fighting aficionado, on his way to the famous arenas in Malaga to indulge his own passion there. He invited me to come along and, for some reason, I trusted him enough to get into the little European car and accompany him for the drive through breathtaking Spanish countryside to Malaga. I can't imagine how else I would have found my way into the experience of such a fight to the death ritual. I learned a lot about bullfighting during that drive to Malaga, how the matador's symbolic relationship with the bull embodies a quest to find immortality. Witnessing this ancient battle of wits between man and beast was brutal. What part of the aficionado's soul was this feeding?

I'm glad I didn't know or particularly care about the outcome of my encounter with Philippe while it was happening. His English was good enough; with my passable high school French, we were able to communicate clearly. But it was an unspoken passion combined with easy camaraderie that paved the path of an extraordinary week spent with this man. We loved with complete abandon. I sat in a restaurant for one of our last meals together, smiling, open, full of delicious food and his presence. He was to leave for his home in Marseilles the next day. I waited silently for an invitation to visit on my way back to London, but it never came. The five-page, hand-written letter that arrived shortly after he left contained only his heartfelt outpourings of love and gratitude for our time spent together, referring to me as his *secret garden*. I realized with a thud in my stomach that he must be married. Our affair was simply a place he could feel alive in secret behind a locked door, hidden from the rest of his day-to-day life.

Where in my life had I, too, been keeping something alive in my imagination but not in day-to-day life?

I wonder about how easy it is to protect a precious feeling and then get stuck in the hiding place. I knew that making art was this precious place for my husband. I believed he hid his passion for art in order to be responsible, for the sake of providing, and for being the husband and father he thought he should be. These were all assumptions, though, never real conversations with the man I loved. One day shortly after we were married, I went inexplicably into crisis, sought counseling, and began to have weekly sessions. My husband would sometimes join me. We had only been married a year. It made no sense to either one of us. We would stroll down 34th Street toward the therapist's office, holding hands like a couple of teenagers, joking that we were going to our "Relationship 101" class together. Even with a promising career as an architect in front of me, I was frozen in a state of inertia. In these sessions, I didn't talk about the fact that I had stopped making art. I didn't share that I had successfully yielded to my husband's talent, that I had done this without his request or knowledge. I didn't realize that we had an unwritten contract, one I had silently crafted and signed without his knowledge before we were even married. I didn't acknowledge that I would be the rainmaker in the family so he could be the artist and paint. There was no room in this contract for my own artistic talent and motivation. None of this was conscious or clear to me at the time. During one session, my therapist led me to articulate a vision for the kind of architect I wanted to be. I didn't have visions of particular kinds of buildings or a type of client I wanted to serve. Instead I said, *I want to create structures that can invite and support individual expression within the whole, and be seen.* Was this ideal vision of making architecture in a secret relationship with my quiltmaking? If so, I wasn't aware of it at the time.

Going off to quilt camp was a way for me to finally enter my own secret garden.

My teacher for the workshop was fiber/quilt artist Joan Colvin. I only knew her from her book called *The Nature of Design*. Whereas my quiltmaking up to this point was inspired by randomly discovered geometric order, her work was all about natural flow and capturing an inspired moment. Sewing straight, even stitches controlled by a machine was what I knew best. The feel of a perfectly finished edge, no frays or loose ends showing, was what I loved to feel. In contrast, Joan Colvin's quilts carried an energy of freedom from these traditional conventions.

My stomach lurched at the very thought of using her favored techniques: raw edge appliqué that features the organic shape of a piece of fabric applied without finished seams, and free-motion quilting, where quilting stitches are added by machine, but with feed disabled and a special open foot that allows hand-guided sewing in any direction on the surface of the quilt.

I couldn't sleep the night before the first class of the workshop. I had arrived at the college campus where the conference was held and moved into my stark dorm room amongst the veteran quiltmakers who had been attending for years. I was there right on time, and surprised to see they were all clearly settled already, at home within the concrete block walls, vinyl tile floors, and old metal-frame beds. Some were already sewing, but they were mostly sitting in one room or another catching up, with cocktails and snacks and lots of laughter. I declined all the friendly invitations to join; instead, I rearranged the furniture in my room, and pulled out my photos, a roll of tracing paper, and colored pencils. I was in the grip of a need to arrive at class more prepared than

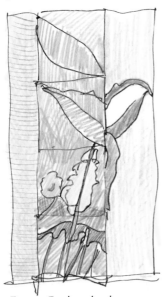

I felt. To feel some control. I moved the photos around on the desk, opened up my field of vision to discover what I was looking for, anxious to explore the limits of my acceptance of where I was. I went to bed with nothing resolved. Sleep was interrupted continuously with that first-day-of-school, butterflies-in-the-stomach anticipation. I finally got up before first light, sat looking at the photos again, ripped off a piece of tracing paper and had a crude diagram drawn within moments. I don't know where it came from, this simple stacking of four images, as if creating a context of thick black

Energy Garden, sketch

50

marker lines for my own internal garden to grow. Like a kid with a coloring book, I added some color, felt the light coming in through the window, and prepared to get to class.

Joan Colvin was gentle and confident, clear and flexible in her offerings. She began with sharing her love of the book, *Bird by Bird*, by Anne Lamott, equating the process of finding voice in writing to finding voice in art. She impressed upon us the value of asking questions and seeing relationships, how by experience, we build our vocabulary for saying what we want to say. I could barely sit still while she finished her presentation, and was the first back to my table to begin work.

The diagram I had drawn became a key for proportionally structuring the elements of the quilt. Each block of color represented a world of detail from the photographs of my garden. I quickly sized the piece of fabric that would be the backing, cut batting of equal size, and pinned both up on the design wall as instructed. We would be building the images right on top of the batting, basting with straight pins, and learning techniques for quilting it all together. The assemblage process was like collage, freehand cutting of shapes and pieces to create the desired image. It was fascinating to see where a template of a flower shape could successfully be repeated, where the uniqueness of a particular shape could serve. Once I got the feel for the rhythm of auditioning different shapes and colors, the quilt took form quickly. Everything got pinned in place right on the design board, through all three layers. By the end of the fourth day I was ready to begin sewing.

Procuring an open free-motion foot for my Bernina sewing machine took a few precious hours that last morning. The process thus far had prepared me to take on this new way of being with a quilt, and I wanted all the relevant tools. The experience of being able to guide stitching in any direction was theoretically exciting, but the reality of being liberated from the strictly forward moving needle was uncomfortable, and it threatened to destroy my sense of accomplishment. I was determined to return home with the feel of how to negotiate fabric and straight pins under the free-motion foot and this required letting the discomfort be an equal participant in the process. I didn't care about fingers getting pricked at the smallest movement, and I finally accepted that there would not be the smooth and comfortable ease of finished seams under my hands. It's not that I muscled through so much as that I finally let go and trusted that something wonderful was happening, even if I couldn't see and feel it yet. By the end of the last workshop day, I pinned my piece back up on the board and stepped back in wonder. There was still a lot of work to do to finish quilting everything in place. But it was a sight to behold, my *Energy Garden*, full of clarity and color, movement and expressive joy, of waking up and asking to be honored.

As I was walking into the dorm of one of my new friends for a celebratory cocktail that last day of class, I called my husband. I couldn't wait to say, *I've found my medium!* In that moment I was no longer the architect responsible for making a living. Sharing with innocence and vulnerability, so inflamed with love for this quiltmaking work, I assumed the artist in him would understand. Instead, he said, *Well, how are you going to make money doing that?* As I felt the knife going into my heart, I snapped my little flip phone shut. It took him ten minutes after I hung up to call back and apologize. But it took years to process the hurt I felt, to come around to owning that it was my fledging trust in who I was as an artist at the time that made me to react with such strength of emotion in the face of my husband's fear.

My husband and I continued to struggle with the marriage. I was fighting for its survival, perhaps even its immortality. After all, my parents had separated and were now back together, forty-five years strong. I was pouring my heart and soul into places that could fill me with love and passion and make me feel alive, hoping that the new growth I was experiencing would reach beyond the walls of my developing garden into our marriage.

I finished the quilt within a month of returning home and promptly hung it on the most prominent wall in the living room. I could see and be with this quilt every day. I had woken up to the strength of creative flow in me while making this piece, and it marked a transition in my life, leading me into the spaces of retreat and reflection that were necessary for the work of growing. The experience at QBL wasn't just about learning new techniques and making new friends. By the end of the week I realized that "quilt camp" was a place where I could practice and devote an entire week of energy to the miracle of art inside me.

When I sit and contemplate this quilt, the stitched lines that radiate and intersect feel alive to me. Many of the flowers wanted their own pattern of stitching inside, while others released their energy to lines that careened right off the edge. It is the combination of these two energies that makes this quilt so vibrant. It is the honoring of both a micro and macro view of the world as experienced from one place. It expresses the desire to be with what is inside while actively participating in what is outside at the same time. It speaks of alignment. When I contemplate this quilt, the energy that holds my connection to the world is no longer a secret to me.

The year after finishing *Energy Garden*, I composed another quilt using the same technique of raw edge appliqué. The focus of this piece was a bouquet of dying flowers, not quite dead, but found droopy and wilted in the vase and then thrown away. What had once been a radiant display of blue-purple tulips, striking daffodils with flowery orange centers, and deep crimson cosmos, was now lying on its side, flowers still clutched together on top of a heap of garden clippings at the edge of the yard. I was mesmerized by the energy that still radiated from this bunch of flowers, clearly still alive, even if discarded. I took a photo and tacked it up on my design wall. I mused about the quality of life of a flower, the cycle of growth and death that came naturally each autumn. I found a few beloved photos of an autumn scene at our country bungalow in the Catskills and as I had found a structure for the forms that became the composition of *Energy Garden*, I produced a sketch for the making of the quilt that would eventually be named *Spent*.

I had come full circle. There was no going back to the traditional techniques I began with. That way, which now felt too exact and finite, was dead now. That death released me to my way, in my chosen medium for making art. My passion to make quilts was more alive than ever. I went on to produce more work in the following three years than I had in the ten before. ❀

Spent, 2004

Reverie

Just as I am falling asleep I see an amazing display of symbols, like hieroglyphics in full color, running as credits after a movie. It is so beautiful. I don't trust that it is real, open my eyes, see that I am in my room, in my bed, looking at the open door just as I left it. Then close my eyes again and the moving images are still there. I want it to slow down so I can really see and remember the symbols, but it is all going too fast. The moving display goes on for some time. When it stops, I fall asleep.

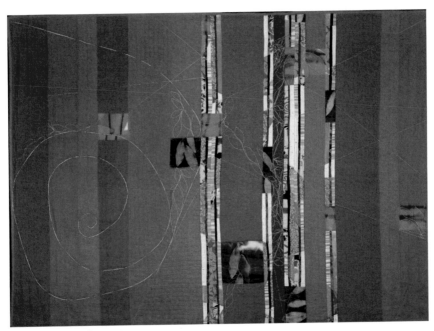

Bar Code in Red, 2005

5

Bar Code in Red

I kept seeing red. All the pieces of red in my fabric stash, yards of red flannel from an unfinished project, the stack of solid red vintage cotton bedspreads found at a flea market. The shades of red were all just different enough from each other to become good textual neighbors. Cutting large sections of each didn't take long at all. For contrast I made similarly sized strips out of different colored scraps, playfully experimenting with thicknesses and patterns of randomly selected fabrics. I had just finished making sun prints of leaves on fabric and incorporated them to help offset the sea of red as well. Putting it all together was fun: fast, easy, and effortless. I would be departing for a second summer week of quilt camp in a few days. I didn't have a lot of time to invest in a longer process and I wasn't taking it seriously in the way I had become accustomed to when engaged with design. I was enjoying the freedom that came with having no expectation of a specific outcome. Making a mostly monochromatic quilt top was preparation for my workshop. I would be learning how to dye thread and how to use it for machine quilting. This red piece would be a perfect ground for practice.

My daughter Molly was twelve years old and had just returned from a rock and roll camp for teenage girls the week before. She discovered her talent for rhythm and composition during her brief time there. Music flowed through her, but she was still seemingly unaware of how it took hold of her, how it changed her from who she thought she should be into someone fully alive in her spirit. In that week of camp, she had been immersed in a world of women making music together and through this, learned about empowerment through collaboration.

She had had her first experience with retreat from what is known and considered safe, into a place that would allow her to refocus on herself and her relationship to music. I was blown away by the quality of song-writing talent that emerged from the girls during their end-of-camp performance. Molly appeared to be comfortable with her achievement. Yet while casually unpacking and getting resettled, she looked at me and in all seriousness asked, "Mom, am I going to have a life?" Wasn't she seeing the brilliance of her own future the way I was? When I said something to that effect, she continued to stare wide-eyed at me and repeated with emphasis, "*MOM....am I going to have a life?*"

It took a few more moments before the impact of what she was try-ing to say hit me. She was referring to her role as Ben's sister, the per-ceived responsibility of being his only sibling, and what that might mean in the future. I thought back to the song she had just written while at camp, which so poignantly expressed the impact of Ben in her life. When she sang the words,

sometimes I wonder
what if my brother was born again
would I look at things differently from my friends
as some can blindfully see
how joyful he can be

I felt tears well up in me, felt her bittersweet awareness of how he had already changed the way she viewed herself in the world. I was so focused on Ben being the different one with special needs that I had tuned out her angst, which lived in all the other verses of her song. With her standing there before me, with the hot need to hear an answer to her question, I faltered. I know I said all the right things to ease her worry, but deep down, she had raised a big red flag for me. I woke up to the future of life with Ben as not just my responsibility. Yes, he might someday be able to take a larger part of responsibility for himself, but he would always be everyone's responsibility. It was time to see how his presence was working on us all. We were part of a relatively small family unit at this point in time. My brother had moved his family to California a few years earlier. My parents and elderly mother-in-law also lived in different states. I began to understand Molly's anxiety. When we can't be fully responsible for ourselves, to what degree can we rely on our tribe for support?

I arrived at quilt camp and spent the hours before class basting the red quilt top to batting and backing in preparation for machine quilting. In contrast to hand basting with thread in preparation for hand quilting, the use of safety pins was a favored technique, stabilizing the three layers of a quilt construction and allowing for quick removal under the running foot of a sewing machine. I didn't know what I was doing; I had never pin basted a quilt for machine quilting, and I relied on the expertise of those around me to learn how. One woman actually gave me her metal tin of safety pins and loaned me the specially crafted, wood-handled tool used to guide the pin from the back of the quilt to the front for clasping. She taught me right there how to do the job with the three layers pinned to the wall. I was learning that this community of women at quilt camp was a family, too. The legacy of quilting was like a bloodline that naturally anchored us in a motivation to share and bask in each other's achievement and creativity. The large red quilt remained on the wall throughout the week as a reminder that I could joyfully share where I was in my progress and accept help when I needed it.

The pull of blood ties seemed to be a theme that summer. While I was learning to make hand-dyed thread, Molly and Ben spent the week with their father at our bungalow community in the Catskills. It was during this week that Molly began her menses, and I wasn't there to share her initiation into one of life's most precious gifts to women. I buried the jealousy and hurt I felt when, unbeknownst to me, a colony friend took it upon herself to mentor Molly that weekend. I should have been grateful, but I was swimming in regret. I should have been there. Wasn't it my duty and right as the birth mother to pass this wisdom on to my daughter? Had I truly come to believe that I was the whole tribe, singly responsible for every important aspect of a child's upbringing and education? Hadn't I just spent a whole week in community in a way that showed me the power of support that grows from shared responsibility? What happened to *it takes a small village to raise a child?*

I'd had an easy enough pregnancy with Molly, happy and full, but I never felt fully connected to her in a way that let me know who was there. She was very late, so long in the safety of amniotic fluid that when she finally arrived, body and soul merging in the swirl of blue light my mother witnessed as she came out of the birth canal, her skin was red and peeling as if sun burned or overcooked. It wasn't until she was placed up on my chest in those first moments of breathing, her face half grimace half smile, that I could feel an ancient heart-to-heart connection with her. She may have waited to become fully embodied during our first nine months together, but in my arms, I felt her presence completely, at peace and suffused with calm that she would struggle to remember as she moved more solidly into life as Molly.

Her entry into this life signaled the continuation of a cycle of births that began with the due date of *sometime late March* that my mother had been given for my birth. Who knows—I might have been a little reluctant too, as I waited to enter the world on April 3. It was Maundy Thursday in the Christian calendar, a full moon, and I emerged at 12:31 pm. The next year, pregnant again, she was given the same due date: *late March.* My brother was born on March 24, Maundy Thursday, at 12:30 pm on a full moon two years after me. My mother told of countless sightings of sister and brother sitting silently together as very young children, holding hands and communicating as two who might be marked by a special common bond. The purely physical expression of our childhood eventually gave way to a kind of connection typified by lifting the phone receiver to hear the other's voice without even an announcing ring. My brother dedicated countless hours to helping me and Molly's father prepare for her arrival, taking the train from Washington, DC to be part of the process. I, too, had been given a due date of *sometime late Ma*rch, and he was convinced that the baby would be born on his birthday. After a number of days of slow, drawn-out labor, he boarded the train one more time the morning of March 24 when it became clear that birth was imminent. He likes to tell this part of the story, how he arrived at the loft where our father waited for him and promptly said, "What are we doing here, let's go to the hospital!" My brother, who loathes exaggeration, maintains to this day that when they entered the hospital, the big, round clock over the reception desk said 9:02 p.m. Molly's birth certificate documents her time of birth as 9:02 p.m. And as she was being cleaned up by the attending midwife, her drippy skin a curiosity, my mother overheard her say to the nurse, "It's funny, it's almost as if she was waiting for something." Molly was surrounded by her grandparents and uncle within moments of being brought to the birthing recovery room. Our own small village. Champagne was uncorked. We celebrated the arrival of the first of our bloodline's next generation.

I didn't dwell much on Molly's waiting for her uncle before rooting herself in this human life. He had developed an early talent for making music and was devoted to immersing himself in Spanish-speaking cultures during his college and graduate school years. By the time Molly was born, his Spanish was so flawless that you couldn't even tell where he learned it. He honed his athletic prowess in all the sports he engaged in. Molly's talent for music began early, too. By the time she was in high school, she also distinguished herself as a star athlete in her sports of choice. It was when she developed her passion for speaking Spanish and exploring Latin cultures that it was impossible to ignore the similarity of her path to her uncle's. It was a thread of lineage that had begun with our mother, who had also studied Spanish in college, also played piano and guitar, also embodied an athletic grace that came through as she danced. Red carries the energy of *blood is thicker than water*.

Practicing what I learned in my week of retreat at quilt camp that summer took me into 2004. Red continued to dominate the work. Red, the universal color associated with STOP long enough to look around and see what is there, what is a danger, what needs to be considered before moving on in a way that feels safe. Red blood, not of this earth directly, but rather born of a chemical process unique to animal life. Blood can absorb heavy emotion and carry it away in a rush to merge back with the earth—through menses, through violence, through life and death. If blood family isn't safe, or if the rules that demand allegiance are too much, one needs to make a choice to stay or leave.

I began quilting by tentatively filling in the strong vertical bars with random pattern. Even as I was covering whole strips with playful machine stitching in thick colorful threads, it felt like an exercise of texture within red, within a code. The red became intense and rich and heavy in feeling, as if I didn't want to color outside the lines or stray too far from what I thought was expected in this linear design. Every colorful stitch contributed to the body of stitches that finally began to balance with the overwhelming red of the whole.

Individual expression was precious to me even as a child, and I'd grown up with the freedom to explore with passion. But I wasn't always rewarded for my choices. Somewhere along the way I learned to fear rejection or worse, what I thought might be excommunication from the tribe if I didn't behave properly. I considered Molly's life-defining moments and her own relationship to individual expression, and I had to reckon with where rigidity and unspoken expectations about responsibility lived in our bloodline. It was while working on the quilting lines over the period of the next several years that the red in this quilt worked on me, helped me see where I could stop responding as if on automatic pilot, where I could begin to slowly stray out from under the umbrella of a blood-based identity without fear of rejection. I could begin to explore a middle ground between what was known and unknown. I started making curves, curves became leaves and vines, and before long, the stitching took on a life of its own. A spiral formed and grew in the

last remaining space of red that wanted to be marked, as if to document how the structure of family, by virtue of its certainty, can help us grow to see who we really are or want to be.

One day the quilt simply became *Bar Code in Red*. First glance at the

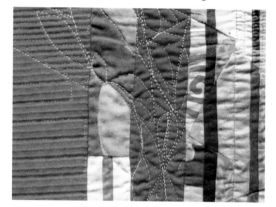

Bar Code in Red, detail

composition reminded me of the kind of bar code imprinted onto objects to mark them with a group identity. But there is nothing about a typical black and white bar code that suggests how something might be unique or different. I began to dwell on the nature of bar codes and the ways we are marked as members of a family or of a certain race or class of human. Eventually, this train of thought brought me back to Ben, his difference, the mark of his Down syndrome like a bar code announcing what category of creatures he belonged to. I had learned to focus on the special needs in front of the abilities that were considered "normal."

I cringe at the memory of a phone call with a friend who was pregnant at the same time I was pregnant with Ben. She called a few days after his birth, saying with enthusiasm, "*Is he perfect?*" I let out a wail and said "*Nooooo!*" What was human perfection? The memory of

Molly's soulful song and the words *would I look at things differently from my friends* appeared and reappeared throughout this train of thought until I realized that *Bar Code in Red* wasn't about highlighting those persons branded with special needs as distinct and different. It was about screaming out loud to STOP and consider that as a tribe of human beings living on this earth, we *all* have special needs and we *all* have abilities, every single one of us. Molly's needs were shaped by her bond with her different brother. Her relationship with him would continue to impact her choices.

There were whole books written about siblings of those with special needs when Ben was born. I didn't read any of them, I was so focused on Ben getting what he needed. Molly was just always there. If she wanted anything beyond what we were giving her, she never indicated so. She was a good girl, easy, quietly taking charge of her life, standing up and walking at ten months old, curious, soulful, never making a fuss. When she was two years old and still just learning language, she woke from a nap, swung her little feet to the floor, looked at me with wide eyes and asked, *Where is Darjeeling?* She embodied the presence of someone who carried wisdom far beyond her years. I simply never worried about her. So imagine my surprise when I went to pick her up at preschool one day and found her sobbing in the lap of one of her teachers. After months of being bossed around by her supposed best friend, she'd finally dug her heels in and said *no*. Actually, what Molly bellowed out to her friend (who had relegated her to the role of frog—again—during make-believe princess playground time) was, "*You make me sick!*" Molly was mortified at her outburst and spent the remainder of the day sobbing. I found her inside with the teacher, who was silently rubbing her back. This same teacher later told me that she had supported Molly right away by saying, "Good for you, for standing up for yourself."

Molly now lives in Peru. She works hard at the life work of finding the middle way between her own bloodline and the ancient one that has adopted her from afar. Her hopes and dreams are bold, accentuated by her choice to identify with and find a life in the space between two very different cultures. She has created the context she needs to practice who she is as a member of both tribes and determine how to maintain her own truth at the same time. Here, she has found her unique musician's voice, and the courage to face where her heart needs to accept difference. Her music has become a meld of Andean tradition with the folk songwriting she found inside herself as a teenager. Her choice has challenged us all to consider where responsibility for each other is embedded in the identity of our tribe.

In 2005, two years after starting *Bar Code in Red*, I was preparing for a group show in which nine of my quilts would be displayed. At the last minute, I decided to include this almost finished quilt, which I still considered just practice. After spontaneously adding a few last stitched lines of quilting and a solid red binding, it was added to the pile going to the gallery. I didn't know where it would hang since my space allotment was already spoken for. After we all worked to hang the show, it

Bar Code in Red displayed

didn't take long to see that this quilt was meant to be displayed on an end panel facing the center of the room.

Here, there was enough space to contain its energy. I stood back in awe, acknowledging the effect of the red holding ground for the rest of the show. In a heartbeat, this went from being a practice quilt to something that wanted to be reckoned with, from being in the background to being in the foreground. I had to accept that this truly was a finished piece, carrying the same weight as all the others, even if its composition was formed in a different way than the family of quilts of which it was a part. ❂

Dream Reverie

I find my cat lying dead on the floor. I put him on a plate and proceed to cut him up and eat him, fur and all. It feels completely right to me. All that is finally left is his eyes, nose, and ears, lying flat on the plate staring up at me, and I know I can't eat those; the thought of that actually makes me nauseaus. I walk upstairs, set the plate down on the floor and walk away, then walk back up the stairs just a few minutes later to find the cat almost completely regenerated, full body and head and half of each of his legs. He is flopping around on the floor and I just stand there watching him, at first feeling the instinct to pick him up and help him, then clearly knowing that I am to leave him alone and that he will complete himself on his own without any intervention from me.

I wake up, heart thumping, but in awe of how natural the whole thing feels to me.

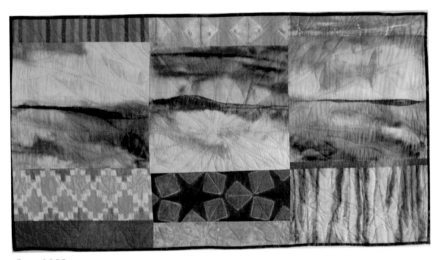

Core, 2003

6

Core

Spring, the season of my birth, was when I consistently felt new creative impulses. Also typically proactive and positive, I resisted giving voice to any worry or fear that lived in me. But when the kids were in preschool and our life was still centered in NYC, strep would descend on me relentlessly each spring. For three years I suffered through a pain in my throat severe enough to leave me completely immobile for days (until antibiotics did their work) before I considered that there might be a pattern. I felt the impact of caring for a child with special needs most acutely during these times. As challenging as the day-to-day mechanics of life had become, I actually loved being with Ben and experiencing his unique way in the world. It wasn't that it was so different from what I had experienced as a new mother with Molly, but my relationship to control had been significantly altered by the shock of his birth, and I was in the process of integrating this change. At the same time, my quiltmaking was showing me that the potential for new beginnings was always available and present. *Was my channel of creativity opening in a new, exciting way that I couldn't seem to swallow?* With strep, it hurt even to talk. I had a high tolerance for pain, but even that changed during these strep throat episodes. It was as if stopping the flow of words made space for me to touch fear that still lived in my core. I had had only one true glimpse of this fear, right in the heart of home, in the loft where I loved living with my family. I don't know if it was an out-of-body experience or just a vision that came from the space between waking and dreaming. But the strength of the terror I felt led me to believe it was a true out-of-body experience.

I had been flying around like a bird, hovering at the ceiling and enjoying views of my beloved home from this perspective, high up in the round turret space my husband used as his studio. I was resting in the painting racks he had built to store his large canvases in order to make room for our growing family. I then flew around to the small living room in the heart of the long rectangular space where we routinely hosted popular dinner parties and gatherings. We were living by the heartbeat of Manhattan in a mutually felt passion for urban life that fueled the early years of our marriage and family life. We made room for visitors who loved sleeping on the pull-out couch right in the middle of it all. I could take a bath in the large claw-foot tub, which was positioned so that, with sliding partitions fully retracted, I could take in the entire length of the loft and look out the large, curved turret windows across Sixth Avenue. It was the quintessential artist's loft, a magic space where we had shared love and fun as newlyweds, playing Scrabble and cards, taking long, leisurely Sunday walks around the city, never wishing for anything more or better—except for the one night, as we sipped scotch and smoked cigarettes over a game of Scrabble, when I was thinking about kids and getting ready to broach the subject. My husband, as if reading my mind, said, "Two would be nice."

I flew around to our bed, screened from the rest of the living space by a series of sliding glass French doors. The large, wood loft bed defined its own room, with two tiers of drawers underneath and a headboard that doubled as storage, too. I saw the forms of me and my husband, him curled on his side away from me the way he liked to sleep, me spooned to the back of him the way I liked to sleep. I hovered and watched us until the visceral feeling of separation, and then terror, hit home. I had to make a choice. To stay where I was, alone and free to fly, or to get back into bed with him, attached. The terror was in thinking I *had* to make a choice. I flew back down into my body, opened my senses to take in the white of his T-shirt filled with his scent, and gently placed my hand on his shoulder. As if grounding myself back into a life

I knew and trusted as *me* could only happen in my attachment to him.

As Ben approached school age, something needed to give. We were facing difficult decisions about his education that would include time consuming advocacy, lawsuits, and no guarantees. The loft had been adapted as much as it could to accommodate the insistent changes that come with growing children, and after years of living an open life, the need for more space and privacy became clear. My husband and I could not agree on a next course of action. We were stuck. We began to spend weekends at our bungalow community in the Catskills. Once I got my hands in the dirt in the country and was able to experience the joy of watching something grow, my love of NYC and our day-to-day life there began to change. And the strep throat that would relentlessly appear each spring finally stopped. The opportunity to move to Amherst appeared, and though it meant separation while my husband commuted back to New York for work, we were finally able to begin our next cycle of growth together.

The strep returned in January 2002. It was just a few months post-9/11 and as New Yorkers recently transplanted, we were still processing the aftershocks from the city that had previously been home. After three years of commuting, and having finally made a deal to leave the loft, my husband was living with us full time. Miraculously, he had moved everything from our beloved loft just a month before the first plane struck the twin towers. Life was full and pulling me in many directions in our new town. The kids were involved in many after school activities that demanded presence. My architecture practice was thriving. I was a member of several community organizations. We were finally cultivating a social life in this new home. But issues with our marriage that we were able to put on the back burner during the years of his commuting were now pressing for resolution.

I knew when I felt the sore throat and achiness coming on fast one afternoon that I would need to see a doctor. In agony with an inflamed throat, I went for the strep test and was sent home with penicillin. I couldn't afford the time to be sick and worked through the slow curve of medicine taking effect. Feeling better enough a week later, I confirmed my participation in a sweat lodge at a friend's home scheduled for the following day, a Saturday. She had built a lodge in her back yard next to a giant fire pit and held regular ceremonies there in honor of her Lakota-born husband, who had recently died. I felt honored to be included.

The healer who threw the water for the ceremony that night led us first in preparing offerings of colored fabric packages filled with tobacco, each enclosing a prayer to the Spirits we would be honoring. The theme he asked us to focus on was *finding order in chaos*. There was a huge fire burning in the pit and beautiful snowflakes coming down. Specially chosen rocks for the ritual were heating in the fire. When the eight of us settled into the classically constructed lodge, a bent wood frame with heavily blanketed enclosure, our hostess began to bring in the glowing rocks one at a time. We were there for a long time, through many rounds of prayers to the Grandmothers and Grandfathers of the East (psychological), South (emotional), West (physical), and North (spiritual). With each round, water would be thrown on the glowing hot rocks and dense steam would fill the space in a way that made it difficult to breathe. I was moved to give up prayers I didn't think I'd ever say out loud or admit to myself. My final prayer to the North, *Thank you for Ben,* was delivered with a clear voice and depth of reverence that felt completely natural. Negotiating the sometimes-difficult road of mothering this unusual child was balanced by the inspiration that came easily in his presence. After years of watching my desire to be seen dive out of sight for fear of rejection or betrayal, I realized that he had been teaching me how to see myself through the lens of my heart's desire, without fear, by simply being who he is and letting the world respond with grace to his own heart-based intelligence.

After all eight rocks had been brought in and all prayer rounds completed, we unfolded ourselves and filed out into the cold night past snow merging with dying flames. We shared a potluck dinner, talked about our experiences, and made space for the magic of the evening to integrate. I fell into a deep sleep that night.

I woke disoriented and not completely in my body the next morning. It took another twenty-four hours, just in time for the beginning of the next work week, for the agony of intense itching to kick in. The psoriasis that had been on the back of my head since I was ten was flaring, extending to my ears and down my neck. Simultaneously, I developed a pain in my chest right between my breasts. I went to work to finish two proposals due the next day. By noon I was scared, the chest pain much worse. Convinced that I was having a heart attack, I called the doctor and went immediately to his office. An EKG showed my heart to be completely normal. He took a cursory look at the psoriasis, offering only that *it looked really angry,* and discharged me with a cortisone cream. I arrived home and noticed that now my tailbone was sore. The area around it was red, hard, and inflamed. I had to finish the proposals. I went to work the next day in a high turtleneck and in extreme discomfort. My left knee started to hurt, and swelling in the arch of my left foot was so painful that I actually started limping. Psoriasis continued to appear symmetrically in patches on my elbows, buttocks, knees, and worst of all, on my hands and wrists. Fingers started to swell.

I finally went home and got into bed. It was now day four following the sweat lodge. My joints began to swell noticeably, knees first. By day five, my shoulders, back and ankles. Day six, forearms. My hands were itching mercilessly the whole time with monstrous sores that appeared on all my knuckles. At this point I gave in. Fear morphed into acceptance of this hideous display. Although I was disappointed with the medical community that didn't really seem to know or care what was happening to me, I was fascinated by the symmetrical order with which the symptoms presented themselves. Finally dropping the illusion that I might be seriously ill was a healing in itself. I now needed the simplicity of myself alone in relationship to this energy moving through me. I sent my family away and entered into the experience I was having. Only after making the commitment to ride it out without fear did I start to get better.

At some level, I knew that Ben coming into my life initiated a quest for living without fear. His way and his presence demanded that I consider other paths, even if it meant leaving my career in architecture. It was as if the inertia of physically leaving a beloved life in New York triggered something deep inside to come to the surface for healing. I recovered from that otherwise debilitating week without any further symptoms or concerns. The experience of becoming one with the pain helped me to see how *separation* can be an illusion. My spirit felt strong. The months following were noticeably lighter. The productivity that seemed to flow directly from a clear creative place inside intensified, and it led me to discover QBL and a context for exploring quiltmaking in a deeper way.

By the summer of 2003, I was fully immersed in this exploration with a growing stash of gorgeous cloth and hand-dyed thread acquired in the past year—Japanese, African, Indian, and bold commercial prints. After just two years of art quilt classes, I was inspired to try new things on my own, not waiting for a workshop to guide me. I felt the call to advance my technique, to become a master quilter. Participating in an art quilt group once a month provided structure, deadlines, and much-desired feedback toward this end. I was working on at least three pieces at any one time: something in design, something in construction, and something in the last phase of quilting.

At the end of the summer, we purchased tickets for the entire family to go on a month-long trip to Australia, leaving in early December. We would be living with my friend Kathy and her family. Kathy and I were still best friends. We had kept pace with each other through the years, having each of our children within months of the other, sharing every intimate detail of our developing lives with copious letters and photos. She still had the ability to hold up a mirror for me to experience my depths and accept myself as few others could, even from halfway across the globe. We shared a similar urge to follow a creative thread, and both found our way into quiltmaking at about the same time. This would be our first time together sharing the developing obsession we both had for this work. What had become the voice of my passion for discovering order was her promise of joy.

I wanted to take something with me that I could work on in Australia, and I decided to compose a quilt featuring some hand-painted fabric panels I had recently made. Three of these panels were painted like a landscape, yellow and blue interchangeable as ground or sky, with distinctive horizon lines that marked the space between the two colors. They were pinned up on the wall in a row, oriented the same way. Flipping the one in the middle upside down, as if unconsciously foreshadowing the rich yellow landscape of the outback I would soon encounter, instantly produced a design with an anchored center. Surrounding pieces of fabric were chosen with the idea of reinforcing and framing the obvious symmetry. That was it. The piece was composed and ready to be sewn together within an hour. After presenting it to my art group for feedback the following week I was given a clear message: *make more like this!* The simplicity and symmetry of this piece seemed to appeal to even my most sophisticated critics, meriting praise. I was surprised by their enthusiasm, and even though I didn't feel connected to it with the same conviction, I was excited to share this developing quilt with Kathy during our time together.

I met Kathy when I was ten years old, shortly after a friend from school that year walked away from me and never spoke to me again. I had been a lone figure standing in the door of the library, watching the back of her retreating figure while she ignored my pleas to come back. There was no argument, no explanation, no reason that could explain this rejection. I don't remember suffering in an obvious way. But I began having mysterious headaches for which no doctor could pinpoint a reason. I needed to begin wearing glasses, and psoriasis appeared on the back of my head for the first time.

Kathy and her family moved into the house next door as all this was happening. I led her to my secret place, up in an ancient birch tree hidden in a field behind our neighborhood, and it took only two hours for us to form our White Birch Tree Club. We were the only two members. I don't remember swearing to lifelong friendship, but I'm quite sure it happened in that sacred space of new beginning. We would spend hours together playing, sharing the world we created for our Barbie and troll dolls. We watched our mothers become friends, and before long our families shared holidays and went on vacation together.

In sixth grade, Kathy and I were in the same class. There were two boys named Tom in the class, and they were best friends, too. One of them asked me to go steady, and I proudly wore his ID bracelet with the innocence of an eleven-year-old. Kathy and the other Tom really liked each other and he wanted her to wear the sign of his affection, too, but Kathy wasn't allowed to accept his bracelet. It felt like a seed of discord had been planted in an otherwise idyllic friendship, placing us in spaces separate from each other that felt awkward. Up to that point, it was as if we were just two Kathys who were inseparable. Kathy's father was transferred the next year and her family moved to Ohio. We stayed connected as our lives began to move along different paths. I felt the impact of the separation, but I didn't have an obvious way to talk about or express my sense of loss.

Early one morning, shortly after we arrived in Australia, I unpacked the quilt top I had prepared, along with batting, backing, and a small case of carefully chosen thread and needles. In the cool morning breeze,

I assembled and smoothed out the three layers on Kathy's large kitchen table until every wrinkle was gone. I loaded a long, thin basting needle with thread and began sewing from the center as I had learned; gathering all three layers onto long stitches, I felt the assemblage smooth and stretch toward the unbound edges even more completely under the guidance of my quickly moving fingers. I integrated the order that felt necessary even in this practical task, basting lines dividing the quilt like a pie, first in half, then in quarters, eighths, and so on, until all three layers could be handled comfortably and confidently as a whole. The strength of all the lines converging together in a concentrated center felt like the sun was living in the heart of this quilt. Each line became a potential expression of an unspoken feeling that could finally find voice; my awe of Ben, my angst at living so far away from my dearest friend, my fear of letting go of a career in which I had invested so much, my connection to Spirit and experiences of synchronicity, which happened with increasing frequency. These lines would be the guides for the final quilting.

I began to quilt with thick, magenta red thread that shimmered in gentle waves flowing alongside the basting stitches. I chose a blue and yellow variegated thread to fill and soften the spaces between the bold red lines. Each section developed into a variety of swells created by even more pronounced curves moving toward and away from each other. I was reminded of the day after her wedding, when Kathy prepared for her departure to Australia with her new husband. The two of us sat in the window seat of her parent's home, weeping. It was then that she began to make waves with her two hands moving together, noting the irony that after so many years of friendship, of following our own unique paths, we were now here in the same place, each married, ready to be mothers, and we would be on opposite sides of the earth from each other. The curves of our mutual trajectories would intersect a day ahead or a day behind, but never again at the same time. So many years of marking time in this strong wavelike fashion with Kathy had now passed, with our lives continuing to intersect even from so far away. The sum of all those waves became a beautiful affirmation of the trust I felt in our connection, no matter what.

The quilt went with me everywhere during that month we all spent together in Australia. It's like a movie now, revisiting the scenes of daily

Core, detial

life that passed through the kitchen, taking it all in from the chair where I would settle in and stitch. From this chair, I could see out all the open windows and doors that had no screens, just warm air hovering on each threshold. It felt exotic to be exposed this way. In her kitchen, we were young girls again, full of the promise of lifelong friendship and of being completely seen.

Our two families became one as we traveled together to exciting places around Sydney. I quilted at the beach, in the mountains, and most memorably, sitting under a tree at her brother-in-law's country home in the outback. I can still feel the hot dry breeze while I quilted for hours, kangaroos dancing in the distance. We were nearing the end of our trip. Kathy and I finally fell completely into the core of our connection while in this remote place; as if taking cues from the kangaroos, we danced to Marvin Gaye in the kitchen while our shocked children squirmed at the unfamiliar sight of their mothers letting go with such intimate abandon.

Molly sobbed inconsolably the whole flight home. She, too, had touched the power of her connection to her godmother, Kathy, as "daughter of the heart." It didn't matter that Kathy and I were from different blood lines and that we had spent most of our friendship communicating long distance. In spirit, we were from the same tribe, moving to similar core rhythms. Being able to truly experience the form of each other's intuitive wisdom and passion during this visit, again as we had as girls and young women, was a gift, now enriched with the present awareness that came with motherhood and responsibility to a committed life. Kathy was about to open her own quilt shop and bring the joy of quilting to a wider community. I would continue my journey with quiltmaking as an artist along a more solitary path. When we parted at the airport, it was with a fountain of new tears and the assurance that our paths would continue to intersect. I finished the quilt shortly after returning home. It was the completion of another chapter of our friendship, the one where we each began to truly live our core essence through creativity in quiltmaking. ❋

Reverie

Gramma is outside right now, determined to clean out my garage, frustrated at my repeated exclamations that John and I have to take most of this stuff to the dump before we can really clean. But John isn't here, and she doesn't understand why she can't do the whole job herself. She vibrates with the possibility of making order, of making a difference, of being useful, of just plain working at something.

What good am I if I can't help, she says.

She is momentarily satisfied with being able to straighten out the woodpile and sweep up the visible debris. I'm not there watching and am bracing myself for whatever else she decides to do. She has already forgotten my request to leave it alone; the disease in her brain that has claimed her ability to hold memory is working full-time now. She's in this present moment of purposeful activity and will simply move onto whatever is in front of her in the next moment. Her need to expend energy is palpable and I let her. The scene of the past and the scene of the future do not exist for her. She is between scenes.

What does one do with such energy when the ability to maintain purpose is gone?

Between Sand & Sky, 2005

7

Between Scenes

I was still exploring the spaces in between primary images of a design. The inspiration for this quilt came from a series of photos of sky and sand, all interchangeable in their subtle variations of sandy beiges and blues. I wasn't paying attention to orienting the photos in relation to each other or thinking I had to make an image that made sense relative to gravity. So I didn't question an impulse to add the image of a large white peony into the grid of sand and blue. It was a compelling image, this peony. We had an entire perennial bed of them, which bloomed every June with breathtakingly large flowers. Each blossom was a profusion of soft, white feather-shaped petals tinged at the center with rich magenta. I loved documenting these flowers up close, filling the entire frame of the camera with their soft vibrancy. Each blossom embodied sensuous energy, beckoning intimacy. It didn't make sense, adding this large, white image to sky and sand, but I did it anyway. I fought for it all the way into the final quilting, determined— even desperate, for no reason I could fathom—to make it work. *Isn't there life in front of and in back of any image? What would that look like?* But no matter what I did, no matter how much energy I put into the elaborate quilting of this oversized white place in the design, it continued to fight back. It just didn't fit. So, one day, I simply set it free by cutting off that end of the quilt. I was now left with a rather uninspiring piece of sand colored fabric framed by bands of blue—bland background at best, without focus.

It was many more months before inspiration arrived again. It's unusual to consider how to further develop a piece that has already been quilted. Typically, stitched lines that bind all three layers of a quilt together signal completion. This quilt had been assembled as raw edge appliqué and machine quilted. I studied the hard lines that both secured each edge of a fabric shape in place and served as a quilting line across the whole quilt. There was a conversation here, something to find in the space enlivened by these lines connecting sand and sky. I began to

Between Sand & Sky, progress detail

cut pieces of fabric to fit just inside the shapes formed by the intersecting lines. The raw edges of these new additions to the quilt were secured with large, hand-quilted stitches using thick, hand-dyed thread, soft and visceral in comparison to the mechanically made machine lines. The quilt transformed. The conversation that was developing felt good. I saw something eerily familiar and, at the same time, incomprehensible, as the sand portion of the quilt became an open center like a portal, letting in all the moments behind and in front to co-exist with the present. I kept filling spaces until it felt done, and experienced great pleasure in the process.

A year had passed since I had brought Gramma MacQueen home to live with us. It was with both relief and disappointment that we moved her to a beautiful assisted living facility nearby after only three weeks. I had been holding onto a different vision of taking care of Gramma. I had wanted her to stay. Shortly after she arrived, I told her we were thinking she could live with us and asked, "How would you feel about that?" She answered, flustered but smiling, "Well, that would be some excitement." I knew she would forget, but, encouraged, I would continue to ask her in other ways to discern if this was the truth.

A few days after this first conversation with her I woke from an intense dream, unlike anything I'd dreamt before. I was walking through a door and as I went over the threshold, an unknown energy beyond my perception and control enveloped me. It felt like two strong, warm arms wrapped around me, holding me where I was at the door. No place to move, completely in the dark, I could only feel. No fear, just acceptance. All day, anytime I thought of this dream, I burst into tears and wondered what, or if, this had to do with Gramma. The thought that kept coming to me was that I had to trust where I was, what I was doing, where it was all leading. I was thinking that taking care of Gramma was part of my path, both for myself and within the family, but trusting that did not come easily. My mother thought that the whole idea of me taking care of Gramma had the feel of impulse buying. Maybe so. No point in saying I didn't feel like I had a choice. Mom was vulnerable and fragile from repeated rounds of chemo and she needed Dad to be available to take care of her; that left neither one of them available for Gramma. Besides, I was one of the few people in the family that could say no to Gramma and hold my ground against her formidable energy. I had such a clear image of making space for her, including a new way to do my work at home. That night I brought up the subject again with Gramma, of her coming to live with us. It's not as if I didn't expect her response of, *it's impossible, old people don't belong in the homes of younger families.* I didn't try to change her mind.

One night toward the end of her stay Gramma started reminiscing about her unhappy childhood. She shed reticent tears. She said life was hard; she didn't ever remember her father being around. She learned to drive at a very young age because there wasn't anyone else after her mother drove the car through the garage. Gramma was the second oldest of six kids and had to work, never finishing high school. She called her mother a saint. But there was something else I could feel her wanting to say. She seemed to be on the brink of telling me what *really* happened, but would catch herself. She got a faraway look and said that her whole life seemed like a big mystery to her right now. Was this the dementia, or just her own reckoning? She asked me if she had done anything bad. When I asked if she remembered her drinking she said yes, but then I told her I didn't understand what she meant by bad.

Was she referring to her reaction when she saw me being kissed for the first time? I was thirteen. We were visiting a new ski resort in the Alps that she was hoping to be involved with in some way as the real estate professional she was. I would have my fourteenth birthday in Paris the next week. It was a glamorous trip. I hobnobbed with an Olympic ski champion and had private lessons skiing through the woods with a beautiful, young male instructor who was also a fashion model. Gramma would take me with her to the discotheque at night, and I would sit with her and her colleagues while they drank and smoked. I recognized the attractive young man who came over to ask me to dance; he was one of the waiters there at the resort. We made it to the dance floor just as the music shifted from rock and roll to a slow-dance song. He pulled me close and held me in a tight embrace throughout the dance. And when the song ended, he leaned his face down and kissed me, a slow gentle French kiss that registered squarely in my belly and made my knees go weak. When I turned and looked at Gramma, she was staring straight at me. She had seen. She knew. And then she started laughing. I learned that I was truly on my own in this arena. We would never speak of my experience, the thrill of being so perfectly kissed for the first time, or of her seemingly callous dismissal of its importance.

I hadn't noticed how much she had been drinking—wine at lunch and dinner, afternoon cocktails, and, of course, the continuously filled glass while out socializing at the discotheque. It finally registered while we were having lunch in a restaurant in Paris a week later. She had just ordered another gin and tonic and I said, "Do you really need that drink Gramma?" Her eyes narrowed in the moment she waited before saying in a quiet, chilling voice, "Don't you ever question what I do again."

Did she think she was bad for not wanting her baby—my mother? Being too young at nineteen to take on motherhood, she had never become a nurturing, caring mother to her daughter like her own mother had been to her. When I asked about her time as a young mother, she referred instead to my mother's huge intelligence, sounding bewildered, as if her own daughter was some creature she'd never understood. She almost let go that night; I could sense the edge of a secret held in for a lifetime. But she was still able to stop herself in time, and didn't tell me.

One day toward the end of her stay with us, I ran a bath for Gramma, left her alone in the bathroom as I had been doing for the past few weeks, and went downstairs to make lunch. I was listening for sounds of her moving around in her bedroom to get dressed. When too much time went by, I went back up and called to her through the bathroom door. She said she couldn't get out of the tub. She was very embarrassed that I was seeing her naked, and she wouldn't let me help her. I finally put a non-slip mat under her feet and she managed to pull herself up. My lord. Now I understood what all the fuss about grab bars was. I also recognized the signal that it was time for something different. I couldn't do this alone.

We moved Gramma to her new home in town. She was independent again and seemed to be happy with the arrangement. Just five minutes away, I could visit her regularly. But it wasn't the same as when she lived in the house with us. Her presence had shifted us all out of a habitual way of relating to each other, had enlivened our family meals, and had created a bigger space within which to experience being our family. Quietly, without fuss or drama, the significance of those weeks she lived with us and the welcome difference it created in our lives fell into the background.

I named the newly transformed quilt *Between Sand and Sky*. The fluidity of the shapes in relation to each other was reminiscent of water and carried the energy of sails in the wind blowing in every direction, across the surface of the quilt, but also down into depths beyond. Inspired by the image and feeling of what emerged, I began to replicate the process in a second quilt. I chose four scenes of sky and horizon, simple formations of cloud, blue, and the myriad colors of sunset and

sunrise. I didn't try to will something unwanted into the composition this time. With a newly felt trust, I simply highlighted the moments I wanted to see with a gorgeous, hand-dyed, golden silk. As with the quilt before, a world was opening up and becoming lighter, less dense, as if frozen moments

Between Skies, 2004

offered a glimpse of something otherworldly, a future in dimensions beyond what I could see, or moments of a past I might have missed. I was thrilled with the feeling of something unknown here. Turning it ninety degrees offered an entirely different glimpse, equally compelling. This quilt wanted to be experienced multi-dimensionally. I called it *Between Skies.*

They were quilts by definition, but not pieces that could endure under any kind of consistent touch. As art, they would be hung on a wall and viewed a certain way. When this second piece was finished, I was left wondering, *what was I making?* These images didn't make sense, yet they embodied a clear feeling of trust for me. The will to keep moving forward, to feel success in relation to my own willpower, even in the face of the unknown, was synching with the powerful presence of Gramma. In the moment of acknowledging that I felt trust here, as with

Gramma in her own process, I could feel myself relax and yield to something unseen.

The energy of the white flower eventually did reappear, though in a very different form. It was 2007. I was participating in a silent retreat at an indoor studio space that had been darkened like a cave. We moved, we meditated, and we slept together in silence over a period of three days. During this time, I had a clairvoyant vision that was as real to me as any object experienced through five earthly senses. Hovering just above me, suspended in motion, was a torus of white feathers attached to a sheath of dark pink that was folded back into the feathers, like a donut hole, a vortex with a perfect empty center. I could see through to open space on the other side. The pink glistened and vibrated like well-nourished tissue. This vision, whatever it was, was alive. I could feel this creature's essence and intelligence and love. I felt the impulse to move though

Between Skies, 2004

its center. I knew I was being offered the opportunity to experience a moment without future or past. The word *stillpoint* came to me. I was frozen where I was, unable to move. The creature disappeared.

Gramma's Alzheimer's progressed steadily and her visits to the house became less and less frequent. Four years had passed since the fall weekend she came home with me. By the time I had left for this retreat, she had been moved to a nursing home, to the wing dedicated to memory-impaired residents. She was challenged to shift even further into a different way of relating to community. I was witnessing how each loss seemed to bring Gramma, gently, to another place of acceptance. With every word lost, her heart compensated. She became a presence beloved by all who came in contact with her. It wasn't long before our primary communication took place through linked hands on walks around the wing.

She died five days after her ninety-fifth birthday, in 2011. I went to the nursing home the day of her birthday and had to feed her like a baby for the first time. As the spoon reached her lips she shifted her gaze and glared at me. The knowing washed through me that she wasn't going to accept this, and I believe that is the moment she decided to let go. My journey with Gramma in this life was over. Except it didn't feel over. As if by transmission, I could see through her eyes how she had helped create the context for our shared spirit to flow in me. Like Gramma, I had become an independent free spirit because I could create a strong home base for myself. A seasoned divorcée at this point, I was committed to community and family life and the making of my nest to come home to. I didn't do it perfectly. Like Gramma, I felt destined to journey without a life partner. I was able to find nourishment in the connections I made, whomever I travelled with and wherever I travelled to. In her final years, I believe the community Gramma created for herself at the nursing home allowed her to keep her heart open and fly in other ways. I had been gifted with the experience of Gramma's compassion and uninhibited presence during that time. I had been touched to the core by the authenticity of her acceptance of who she was as she graciously allowed herself to be taken care of, making that choice over and over again in each present moment.

I recently participated in another silent retreat. This retreat was fully outside, in the glory of mountain and forest during a beautiful, crisp fall weekend on the cusp of a full moon. It involved camping out with a like-minded group, contained within a mutually maintained silence, with alternating periods of sitting meditation and challenging hiking up a mountain and back. The trails were difficult. This became evident soon enough, as bold faces of stone began to greet us, asking to be climbed. Conversely, the forest provided a sweetness of green and light-filled protection during sitting meditation, until the elevation was just too high for sustained growth. Then we were led out onto broad expanses of ancient stone to bask in the kind of silence that comes with seeing so clearly, such a broad section of the earth beyond and below. Being in silence and in open attention to every sensation was exhilarating, even fun after the challenge of the climb. But the joy of the moments spent at the top quickly dissolved into the physical pain in my knees and legs on the descent. I had to move slowly, while the rest of the world seemingly bounded past me with ease. I had to find the place in me that could yield to the pain instead of expecting the mountain to yield for me. As I slowly walked the last few hundred yards into our campsite and saw the rest of my group, I was filled with a peace that flowed into me as easily as the pain flowed away.

It wasn't until the next morning's group meditation around the fire that I was able to fully embody the seamlessness of moving from pleasure to pain to peace the day before. As if summoned for this very purpose, the image of my feathered vortex appeared. The invitation to pass through the center was still there.

Maybe this was the spirit of Gramma inhabiting a form of eternal return. Maybe I could rest in time with this creature and honor my desire to get to the other side of some unimaginable future. Or maybe its very essence was structured in such a way as to allow the fleeting, transitory experience of every desire to pass through, and then be forgotten. ❈

Reverie

I wake realizing I love myself in my pleasure. Pleasure in moving my body to a force I can't control. I walk to the lake and sit in a chair facing the glow of almost sunrise. Only the bird song, the incredible space surrounding just me. I close my eyes and enter into this amazing sensation, the entire center of my body wide open, waves from my heart to pit of my belly and back. Electric, so amazingly pleasurable. The feeling of being loved underneath it all, knowing that I am loved. And the sun pokes up over the ridge and I hear life waking miles away, so close at the same time. Truly happy to be just me where I am right now.

Cave Jewels, 2006

8

Cave Jewels

The flea market in downtown Sydney was wide open, tables spread out in the shade of park trees, out of the hot sun of December 2003. I was still pinching myself that we were actually here for the much-anticipated month-long visit with Kathy and her family for the holidays. Having just arrived, we were in that sweet spot of a visit, acclimating to the new time zone and culture on this other side of the planet where it was summer, not winter. We had a long stretch of planned fun ahead, and it was significant that we would blend our families for this time and make memories. It was only our second

Fabric Detail

day here and we were already out hunting for fabric.

I saw the wild colors out of the corner of my eye and made haste to the table that held a spotty collection of things. Staring down at bright and bold and full of life, stripes of a tiger meets Marimekko, I knew this fabric promised to be something truly distinguished in a quilt. I didn't hesitate to pay the modest price for this abundant two-yard cut; then I turned and shouted out like a little kid to Kathy, *"Look what I found!"*

It was months after our return home before I attempted to honor the strength of spirit in this cloth. There was a force to reckon with here. This fabric held the energy of strong, wavelike flow. I found myself taking pictures of different sections of it just to capture the essence of

Cave Jewels, progress detail

this movement. My desire to carry the boldness led me to make an initial block, large and colorful, but otherwise uninspiring.

With determination, I kept making them; four was what I had in mind. But it wasn't enough to move with the flow of what was there.

The call to provide an equal and opposite response to what I was seeing and feeling prompted a working title of *Crosscurrents* before the semblance of a quilt was even up on the wall.

The trickle of design finally stopped after I had muscled through four of these blocks. I can't explain why. I was sure four was the right number. I made an attempt at a composition. I could continue to push through, demand a response by virtue of my determination, or I could stop and watch for where the flow was going. I could simply wait. After a few months, I finally let go of whatever I thought *Crosscurrents* meant,

took the large blocks down off the design wall and with intuition guiding my hands, cut them up into smaller pieces. All previous ideas vanished as squares formed from the recombined patchwork pieces. Now I had something to work with. Moving the pieces around like players on a chessboard, I made design decisions fueled by trust and swift

Cave Jewels, progress detail

action. In no time at all, the structure of the quilt took on a whole new geometry of nine squares, and I found comfort in the predictability of structuring the quilt around a clear center. But instead of honoring the directness of the implied form, I still felt guided to celebrate four equal parts. Not a subtle blending within a dominant nine-square geometry,

Cave Jewels, progress detail

no; these four parts needed to assert themselves in a surprising way. They needed to come into the light. Like jewels revealing themselves after having been buried in the fabric of their culture, the edges of the four blocks dissolved into rough cut circles that required space around them to be fully seen. The rectangular pieces were made even smaller to contrast with what was emerging.

With hand-stitched reverse appliqué, sections of bright white fabric were inserted into the space between object and the ground from which it came. It was a feeling of emergence. I took my time, enjoying the process of this liberation. The new name of the quilt, *Cave Jewels,* was born. Jewels present and glowing after being hidden for too long, ready to be touched and experienced with pleasure. Each had its own space and individual glow, but they were all clearly of the same tribe.

I accentuated each jewel equally with radiating echoes of machine made quilting on the outside—thin, hard lines of silk—and hand quilted them inside with thick, white stitches that emphasized rotation around each of the four implied centers. I spent two years, on and off, working on this quilt. It was completed in the summer of 2005 as I was preparing to begin a four-year training in Energy Medicine.

It was only since Ben's birth that the awareness of healing with energy had come fully into my consciousness. The call to this work felt old, even if it presented as a new path to follow. Ben had developed pneumonia within a month of his birth. I knew that the healer my mother had recently started consulting was working on him energetically from her home in another city during his hospitalization. Mom had arranged a time for us all to meet her and do energy healing work with Ben in person three months later. He was okay, but pale and sickly following the assault on his vulnerable three-week-old body from spinal tap, X-rays, antibiotics, and the loud, sterile context of the hospital. It was while in the car driving to the healer's house that I knew this meeting would be my introduction to the work of energy medicine. I was to honor the healer in me. I can remember the feeling of the vibration even now, like a breeze moving through to signal my initiation. It was that simple. Whatever shock I had experienced at Ben's birth, and the subsequent months of adapting to the truth of who he was, was absorbed in this new awareness.

Imagine having just held your beautiful new baby boy. The imprint of joy left by his little body is still there, despite the premonition that all was not as it should be, as he made a strange movement with his neck to turn up and gaze at you. Love, registered fully and completely, is coursing through your body and at that moment, the pediatrician walks in and announces that your son has Down syndrome. The shock, the sheer disbelief of hearing something so unexpected, sends you flying off your bed, so completely out of body that it takes three people to hold you in place.

The training in energy medicine I received was designed for the *wounded healer* with a presupposition that even in the most loving and harmonious context for growing up, our sense of individuality in the world arises through wounding that occurs first in the process of separation from our mother. Given this, the training first required years of discovering where patterns of self-defense against the pain and suffering of this separation were rooted in my life.

Just a few months into first-year courses, I had an experience that left me writhing in tears on the floor of our classroom. We were engaged in a simple exercise our teacher had learned from a body of work called Continuum. We were lying on our backs with the intent of moving slowly, spontaneously, and organically to a piece of music. Feeling pleasure from the breath of air on my skin everywhere in the sensuousness of this movement was unexpected. It was a strong flow and I wasn't prepared when our teacher turned off the music and said that it was time to stop. My sobs came careening to the surface with an unstoppable force. I knew that something important was happening, as if I had been suddenly knocked off a horse just as I was feeling the pleasure and certainty of my seat.

Imagine being a first-year graduate student in a renowned institution pursuing a professional degree in architecture. It is the night before a final presentation of a design project. It is late in the large studio bustling with the fervor of beating a deadline, of doing the very best you can do. Your professor appears late in the evening, casually strolling through with some unfathomable purpose. He sits down at your desk, spreads a piece of tracing paper over your final drawing that has already been inked on Mylar, a design that has been produced with so much pleasure, and begins to change your design with wobbly thick lines made with his fat black marker. The flow of accomplishment you were just feeling is abruptly halted. Presentation time is only hours away. Is he actually suggesting that the project be redesigned, now, with just hours left to prepare? The violation that he is perpetrating, the horror you register, sends you fleeing from the studio just moments after he leaves. You find a dark corner of an unoccupied room and pass out from the shock to your system.

Shaken and spent after a weekend of processing the emotional flow that had been initiated, my body simply shut down again. I went home and registered for the first workshop I could find with the founder of Continuum, Emilie Conrad.

I'll never forget meeting Emilie for the first time. She was a strikingly beautiful woman in her seventies, vibrant, warm, with a directness that felt at once personal and universal. It was Easter week and Emilie had structured the work of the week around the experience of death and rebirth. I felt the spotlight of her gaze into my beginner's mind, inviting me to suspend whatever disbelief I had about resurrection as I walked through the door to the space that would be our cave for a week. After group introductions, she asked each of us to share a first awareness of consciously feeling energy moving in our bodies. I don't remember what I said, but Emilie turned her intense gaze on me and asked, "Did you feel pleasure?" I went blank and thought, *What does pleasure have to do with it?*

The work we were led into that week was deep, intelligent, dramatic, and familiar in a primal way. Emilie was teaching us how to use sound to prepare body tissues for opening to the flow of life force through the fluid body. On the surface, it all seemed a bit bizarre. The sounds we were instructed to make came from recesses in the body that felt ancient and primitive: deep sounding Os that reverberated in the chest like a ping pong ball and higher pitched Es pushed through the teeth produced vibration in the throat in a concentrated way that felt like a flood washing away the only language I knew. Making these sounds while placing intent on a specific place in the body produced a kind of reverberation that felt exquisite and entirely new. After many rounds practicing in this preparatory way, we were led to rest in *open attention,* allowing us to consciously track resultant sensations and vibrations in the body and oh my, did this ever feel good! Eventually, my body responded to the pleasure. Suspended, moving ever so slowly into curling spiralic shapes I couldn't even imagine making at will, I felt completely alive to the moment. I wasn't doing it. It was doing me. It didn't take long to feel like I had walked into a world that every cell in my body already knew about intimately, even if I didn't.

Continuum offered a way to have an embodied experience of the universe through the path of spirals. Emilie was teaching from her own experience about how the spiral, as an initiator of movement, is coded in the very DNA of every tissue in the body. She demonstrated the exquisite path a spiral could take in her own body as she opened to the unknown, just as she had been preparing us to do for ourselves. She taught by transmission, offering her own surrender to the process, visible for us all to experience as she moved. The thing about the spiral is that it has no end. It has the quality of uncurling from a dense anticipatory place to an undifferentiated open space with no limits. Emilie referred to the flow that can follow this path as *moving medicine* and we, in our openness to the flow, were becoming *health artists*. What she modeled for us by transmission was movement that had no predicted course—exquisitely beautiful and powerful movement that even I, the witness, could feel. Significantly, she taught that movement through parts of the body that might be closed to this flow of life force can act as initiation for release and healing. Moving medicine had the power to sweep through past trauma and make space for something different.

Imagine being four years old and sitting on the couch with your beloved paper dolls. Your little legs, clad in brand new black stretch pants, extend straight out in front of you, the book of paper clothes, with the little tabs that you can fold onto the doll, sitting on your lap. You pick up the scissors and begin on another outline—oh, this is so much fun! The pleasure of cutting flows through your little hands as your eyes focus on the raised seam of the new pants that is right there alongside the book. What is this? I wonder what will happen if I cut this too? And you do, and then in joy call out to your mother to show her the beautiful hole that has formed. But she is furious that you have ruined your pants and puts you, crying and terrified, alone in your room clad only in a nightgown. She takes away all your other clothes, and leaves you there for the rest of the day.

I gifted *Cave Jewels* to my second-year classmates in energy medicine school. We decided that the quilt would belong to the class and travel amongst us as needed. Together, we imbued the quilt with our group energy and sent it home with the first person who expressed need for a tangible reminder of our community spirit. It would continue to be passed around in this manner. The quilt had become a symbol for the support that we felt in love and in commitment to the healing we shared with each other. I continued with Continuum workshops and practice throughout all four years of my training. The need for individual accomplishment still lived in me, even while I experienced how common—even sacred—purpose could eventually reveal itself through the process of making community. Was there such a thing as relational accomplishment? What power might be released and available for the health and well-being of all people inhabiting this living breathing planet if our individual accomplishments could coexist with a shared sacred purpose? Sacred purpose, for me, was the commitment to create context for the experience of unity, whether with just one other person, or with an entire community. Would it be enough to be just another member of humanity, accepting my humble part without needing to distinguish myself as special?

Imagine sitting in a cafe in the heart of New York City, gazing out a window at the dense flow of people walking the streets. You are in the middle of a silent retreat that has taken you out of the cave of Continuum practice and community, back into the life you have retreated from. You have not spoken a word in the past two days. Your attention comes to rest on a street cleaner who has stopped to attend to the garbage can just outside. You watch him work, as if in slow motion against the rush of anonymous passers-by. You appreciate the pride and satisfaction you feel in his gestures, for keeping your shared context clean and litter free. You feel this deeply. Could this be pleasure? He finishes his job there, picks up his bucket and broom, turns and begins to walk toward you as you continue to sit and watch. As he passes, he looks through the glass straight into your eyes and smiles, as if to say thank you. Thank you for being present here with me and for sharing your appreciation. It is a shock to feel the magnitude of empathic space that has been created between the two of you.

Cave Jewels is a traditional quilt in most ways. It brings many diverse pieces together in a structure that can celebrate individual differences. It is imbued with time and love in the many seen and unseen stitches of appliqué and hand quilting. Its finished edges invite touch with the sensuousness of something that just feels good. It was designed as an art quilt, to be hung on the wall and viewed. After years of being passed around, washed, and held in laps, it can still be hung and viewed from afar as an individual accomplishment of this particular artist. But its real power lives in the relationship that community has added to this piece. For me this quilt is a living testimony to a community that continues to struggle to create space, structure, and support for individual accomplishments made in joy.

When I was preparing to write this chapter, I put out a request to have the quilt returned to me. It is not hanging on the wall. It is draped over a chair where I can see it from most places in my house; at the same time, it's accessible to touch. It continues to carry the energy of stability in community, while simultaneously inviting conversation about the value of something as soft and timeless as an empathic moment. ❉

Reverie

I feel the spiral propelling me to move toward THERE. I am impeccable in my attention to the sensation of the spiral in my body. I enter into a gorgeous association with what is THERE. I become both the message and the messenger.

I am my broken heart.

Storm Goddess, 2005

9

Storm Goddess

I was being courted for junior partnership in the architecture firm of my early career when I became pregnant with Molly. After she was born, I took a standard three-month maternity leave, unpaid. When I worked my way back into a full-time schedule, I asked for a meeting with the partner who had become my mentor. I expressed my desire to continue along the partnership track. His response was, "But you are going to have another child aren't you?"

I buried my shock at the blatant discrimination. I forgave the man I had become so fond of for asking this question. I rationalized that he was old-school, exactly the same age as my father. His wife had raised his children and made space for his career. He didn't understand that my husband and I would be different. He was right, I *was* thinking about having another baby. *So what?* It never occurred to me that I wouldn't pick up and move forward from where I was on my career path before Molly was born. *Why not?* The buried shock festered. I finally received the call a few months later from this same man with whom I had shared such mutual respect. He told me that the firm had chosen to make one of my male colleagues in the office the next junior partner, the one who didn't have children and wasn't planning on any, either. I felt the rug being pulled out from underneath me. I felt mostly numb, but there was anger there, too.

I threw myself even harder into the art of making things. Unlike architectural design, which enlisted the gift of my brain for making things, the visceral and tactile aspects of making things with my hands became a balm for the anger. Except unbeknownst to me, this balm was simply a Band-Aid for an anger that kept spiraling out of sight. The deeper the anger went, the more I rationalized that the man-made, mind-made constructions of architecture were not as heartfelt in spirit or as significant as those things I was making with my hands. I had lost trust in my chosen profession and continued marking distance between me and the work into which I had channeled so much passion over the past ten years.

Wasn't *man-made* the result of an idea that becomes a finished material object? Didn't *man-made* often encounter massive resistance to its physical manifestation, requiring in reaction a kind of persistent hubris in both design and production? Hadn't I realized that *man-made* often required ruthless choices when making something visionary, choices that produce massive amounts of waste? Couldn't *organic*, on the other hand, follow a less resistant, more natural flow to a predetermined, even if imprecise, conclusion? I was learning that staying open to the awareness of *organic* could result in a greater degree of discovery and flexibility in the design process. I felt like my life depended on it. The instinctive impulse to follow this path of discovery during my years of architecture school had now found resonance in a conscious way of day-to day-creative work as mother and artist.

The impulse for the design of *Storm Goddess* began with a nautilus crystal I had found in a shop while visiting the coast of Maine. I photocopied the crystal, enlarged the image, and began to explore the relationship between two spirals. Eventually, I abandoned the certainty of what was appearing in favor of a process that would let me discover re-

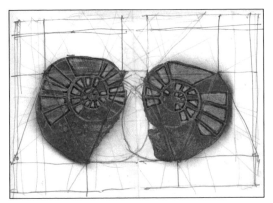

Storm Goddess, progress sketch

lationships in fabric as they developed. I sketched over the lines that delineated clear shape in a single spiral. Each proposed piece was numbered to a master diagram. The overall image for each block was quite large, twenty-six inches by thirty-two inches. I determined to make four of them, and chose a palette of fabrics to incorporate a full range of value from light to dark. I loved working with the newly acquired speed and confidence of raw edge appliqué. But I was still attached to the traditional process of sewing one piece of fabric to another to produce smooth, finished seams in a way that signaled mastery and tradition. Making these blocks was going to be hard. The construction of the spirals wanted a precise process. I chose the stacking

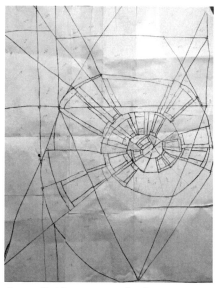

Storm Goddess, progress sketch

and cutting technique from my earlier quilts to accomplish this. Because there were so many pieces in each spiral block, some of the fabrics got placed in a stack two or three times, resulting in more cut cloth than I needed. The waste was put in a large container, the beginning of a scrap bin that would figure heavily into my future work.

The order of each block became more and more visible as I worked. But maintaining this order in a competent way with so many curved pieces challenged me. How long would I be able hold to the precision I expected in composing these cleanly pieced seams? Polished man-made objects represented centuries of human beings growing and evolving with the products of sophisticated technology. I grew up with the promise of a better life as a result of industry and standardization. But after years of dumping disposable diapers into the garbage, I had developed a natural aversion to creating what felt like excessive waste in exchange for time-saving convenience. I began to feel panic at the thought of the waste footprint produced by my one little family of four. And it made perfect sense to me that there would be a direct relationship between waste produced in manufacturing and the health of human beings exposed to polluted air, water, and earth. The green movement in architecture had been manifesting in the establishment of sustainable practices, means and methods for making the major man-made constructions that created context for our cities and communities in an ecologically responsible way. It would have been the most natural thing in the world for me to follow this path, and embrace the industry curve of these practices into sustainability. But I resisted even this. I wanted to continue living in a context that allowed for mystery and spirals into the unknown to be the guiding force for life. I wanted to make another baby. I wanted another sibling for Molly and Ben. I wanted to yield to the force that was moving me intuitively away from everything that I thought I desired as a young woman.

When Ben was just a few months old and I was still carrying him around in a sling, I would put Molly in her stroller and the three of us would walk to our neighborhood playground at Union Square. I was surprised to find my favorite architecture professor there with his young son one day. He was old enough to be the boy's grandfather. In fact, he too, like the partner in the firm who had recently been my mentor, was exactly the same age as my father. When he was my teacher at the Institute of Architecture and Urban Studies during college, he honored my intellectual curiosity and encouraged me to keep asking questions. I was lucky enough to study with him again in graduate school during his three-year post as a visiting professor there. That year, I was the only woman in his class. He praised my project and at the same time said, "this is the work of a repressed woman." He had become one of the world's most acclaimed architects, famous for the intellectual rigor that infused his work, and he had influenced me as a student of architecture more than anyone else, consistently creating a context for me to dig deep into my motivation for discovering order. Now, with my baby wrapped tight to me, I shared with him who Ben was while Molly and his son played together. He was quiet for a moment, looked straight into my eyes and said, "Well, you need to surround him with siblings." It didn't feel like a sexist remark. It had just felt true.

I was now forty-five. Ben was ten years old and all discussion with my husband about having another child had died years ago. I did not have amniocentesis when I was pregnant with Ben, and my husband was clear: he couldn't face another pregnancy without the test. It was impossible. The thought of aborting a child who might be Ben haunted me. My resistance to letting go of the possibility of another child hovered the entire time I worked the path of curves in these blocks.

How long would I dwell in the tension between expectation and desire before surrendering to a freer, more intuitive way through raw edge appliqué?

This pattern of the nautilus had presented a clear opportunity to engage. I was attracted to the universal order that lived in this form, free from stereotype and branding. Here was order that guided the growth of men and women alike. It was order that held no judgment of precise finished seams *or* flowing raw edge, being a mother *or* being a professional. The structure of spiralic growth that is always there, just waiting to be discovered and experienced, was pulling me into the design. I was seeing spirals in every flower, feeling their presence in every rock. And even if I couldn't actually feel the most subtle form of this energy yet, I knew these spirals were present in the molecules of the matter I connected with every day, in the very DNA of my own human body. The creation of form through naturally occurring organic growth was beautiful in its simplicity *and* beautiful in its complexity.

As an architect, I was well-trained to discern the difference and strive for a balance of economy that would allow characteristics of both simplicity and complexity to be accessible through design. But I had never consciously considered how my own DNA as a woman might possibly pre-dispose me to experience a process of organic growth differently than a man. By now, my ability to nurture growth in the womb and give birth to another human being was established. This ability distinguished me and I knew, with unshakable certainty, that it was something that would challenge my continued growth as a professional. Would there ever be an acceptable balance between mother and architect? It wasn't until the birth of Ben and becoming the mother to a child with special needs that all bets were off. Mother trumped architect.

And then I met Albert. Just as I was beginning the work of *Storm Goddess,* he hired me to create a roadmap for the renovation of his historic house. He would be developer and builder and the presence at home for his children while his wife maintained her full-time job. I made it clear that doing this kind of work required me to learn the daily flow of a household. He didn't hesitate to invite me to spend time with his family; he opened his home to me, and we became colleagues and friends in the process. Mother and architect became one in my relationship with this man who intuitively understood exactly how to tap my unique combination of skills and talent.

As we were nearing the time of construction he called to inform me of a change in the master bedroom suite that would need to be made, so that it could accommodate a nursery. His wife was pregnant. As he shared his excitement about their news, I felt a strange, knowing, wave pass through me. When he called a month later to tell me that they had just received the results from an amniocentesis, that the baby had Down syndrome, the wave returned and deposited the weight of its crash in my heart. That night I woke as if from a dream and heard the anguished cry of Albert, *But I have to protect her!* He had wanted to keep the baby even though he and his wife together had made the decision to terminate the pregnancy. His cry was like a blade severing the lock of an ancient secret.

Sewing each of the four blocks for this quilt was proving to be a worthy challenge. I'd get up in the wee hours while the rest of the house was still asleep and sit at my dining room table with the hundreds of pieces begging to be sewn together, angles joined to curves in provocative ways that tested the limits of my skill. I had to work and rework many seams to find the exact place that the curves would lay flat. My obsession with the order of something perfectly executed continued to reign. An underlying discomfort began to unwind with each finished spiral. What if I let go? As if mimicking the slow progress of growth that one might expect in nature, I couldn't force this part of the process, and each block took a long time to complete.

Once they were done, off the table and pinned up on the design wall, a completely different kind of viscerally palpable energy took over. This phase of the work took place in the seclusion of my small upstairs studio, where I kept my fabric and meditation cushion, where I could sit at length, contemplate, and take in the full measure of a developing composition. Seeing the four spirals rotating in relation to each other, a wild, rhythmic, swirling dervish kind of a dance developed. The

Storm Goddess, detail

composition came out of nowhere and everywhere, and because it was happening so fast, I knew I would now have to accept raw edge appliqué as part of the process and let go of the purity I still associated with finished seams. The soft colors, even the abundance of pink, couldn't mask the sharp and almost dangerous sense of being unleashed that was developing.

Something was working through me even if it wasn't touching *me* yet. I was excited by what I saw. I was making art. I was inspired. Detached. I don't remember feeling pleasure. I decided to maintain the fast pace of construction with machine-quilted lines and curves. It was bound and finished in just a few days. The title of *Storm Goddess* came with clear force. It didn't make sense at the time. It wasn't until much later that I felt the significance of the energy that lived in these words: *I needed to destroy something.*

At last, I could look directly at the twenty-one-year-old honor student I was in college, bound for graduate studies in architecture and a promising career, pregnant and faced with an impossible choice. For years I couldn't take responsibility for the decision I had made to terminate. At first I believed it was my mother who convinced me that having the baby would ruin my life. That marrying the man who fathered this child would be a big mistake. That I was too young, with my whole life ahead of me. That I could never tell him. She never stated the obvious source of her counsel, that she had married my father when she was my age and had given birth to me when she was just twenty-three. Life hadn't worked out for her the way she had envisioned when she was my age. She was a brilliant mind, a gifted child prodigy and successful college student, beautiful and accomplished, destined for greatness. She had wanted to go to law school, perhaps even be a judge someday. She wanted me to have the chance she never had.

Alone in my room, awaiting the dreaded appointment that would end the pregnancy, lying on my bed in a forced sleep to blunt the shock of what was about to happen, I was haunted by the image of the little girl who came to me in a dream. She appeared as if the most natural thing in the world. She was about three or four years old, with wise eyes and a presence that opened the space for me to see the choice I had already made all by myself, regardless of my parents' input and advice. I had already rejected a relationship with the baby's father because of my ambition and desire to pursue a professional career. I wasn't ready to change my mind about this on the basis of one passionate night.

My father sat me down just before my mother would arrive to take me to the doctor's office, looked me in the eye and asked solemnly, *Are you sure?*

No, said the scared little girl buried deep inside me, now standing alongside the image of the little girl whom I was letting go. It was a perfect swirl of conflicting intentions. It didn't feel like a choice, even if I had made it. As if standing in the eye of the storm, I absorbed the shock with calm and resolved to put it all behind me.

Yes, I said to my father. *I'm sure.*

In retrospect, I see where anger moved through this quilt. But it's hard to siphon off, to separate it from the love that is there, too. *Storm Goddess* was holding a spiral of conviction that began with innocent conversations as a girl—with being twelve years old, sitting across the table from my father, asking why he had decided to become a dentist. He had been so clear in his response, so confident. I asked, "How do I decide what I want to be?" He said without hesitation, "What is it that makes you happiest?" I said, "Making things with my hands!"

Even at twelve, I already had a rich history of making things with fabric, making clothes and gifts, writing stories—anything creative that allowed me to become so absorbed that I lost track of time. The idea of pursuing design was a natural conclusion to these experiences. When I presented my father five years later with the idea of becoming an architect, he nodded approval and said, "That's good, that's something you can do at home."

In acknowledging a focus for my developing passion in the world, while at the same time naming what would ultimately become more important to me than anything (my own family), my father had intuitively hit the nail on the head with his praise. I would be best served by work and a profession that I could balance with my home life. I understood that my father simply wanted what was best for me.

Storm Goddess led me to a place where I could feel the impact of the choice made so many years ago. Anger born in the conflict was still there, swirling inside the trajectory of my life's experiences; it hadn't found a way out until now. Like tearing open a wound that had already healed, I would have to experience pain before I could get really mad. When the pain finally came, triggered by the pressing desire for another baby that no longer seemed possible, it catapulted me into a fearful place that had me questioning every choice I'd ever made. The relentless questioning always began with, *Was I following my heart or not?* That eventually led to the question, *What right do I have to choose me?* The anger finally burst free. It was a gentle release. It felt like a death. I was sad, finally ready to grieve. Healing energy had followed an organic path that brought me to this moment exactly when I was ready for it. *Storm Goddess* had aided in the destruction of energy that was no longer useful. At some point, I would have to accept and forgive myself for the choice I made. But for now, it was enough just to feel.

Storm Goddess now lives in the home of a dear friend who has been a hospice nurse most of her life. She is a brilliant agent for the dying, for those who are poised to let go and gracefully transition to the next place. She recently shared that when she settles into contemplation with this quilt, for her, it simply evokes peace. ❀

Dream Reverie

I am in a healing circle, about fifteen to twenty people, and we are instructed to close our eyes and hold out our hands to "receive" from the healers whom we are there to "see," and yet we are told explicitly not to look. I sit with eyes closed, my hand up and open and feel the lightest touch on my left palm. I wait a moment, then open my eyes to see the heads of this very tiny couple, man and woman, on the other side of the circle, she with long white hair, he with short white hair, exactly the same size, moving in unison together around the circle. I realize they are healing together as balanced masculine/feminine. I allow myself to really look then, as they are finishing, while most of the others leave without looking as instructed. The woman is now standing in front of me, looking at me, smiling. She begins to move my body parts kinesthetically in exploration and I am thrilled that she has chosen me to work with more deeply. When she is behind me moving and bending my torso, I look across at him, talking happily about going out and getting beer as if we are at a party, looking at her with indulgence and reverence at the same time. She turns me to face her, and instead of telling me what she has found, she lets me do the talking. I tell her that I know of the wound in my heart, but don't know what it is, what to do about it, or how to release it.

Diamonds in the Rough, 2005

10

Diamonds in the Rough

Diamonds in the Rough is a large, bed-size quilt made from pairs of strip-pieced squares, each cut in half and sewn to the companion of the other. I had made simple patterns for cutting multiple layers of fabric in stacks. Then, I randomly chose pieces from each stack to comprise the initial pairs. I made a free-form diagonal cut through the two, fitting one half of one to the other half of the other in a perfect match. Not the romantic kind of match, where there is only one perfect half that fits with my half to make the whole. No, this was a validation of the infinite ways my half could fit with another half and form a beautiful partnership. The seam between the two maintained the subtle curve made with one swift motion of a rotary cutter. What emerged was a juxtaposition of colors and textures that inspired me to make lots of blocks and imagine how the curves could connect in a larger whole. It felt right to make something big. This process yielded double what I needed for one quilt. The idea of putting the unused halves away for another time also felt right.

It was 2005, and we had been living in Amherst for seven years. The architecture partnership that brought us here was flourishing. My new partner, twenty-one years my senior and firmly established in the community, had given me free-reign to be the competent professional I was. With his support, I quickly established my strong voice as an advocate for affordable housing in existing historic structures that could be renovated. I honored my partner. I thought he was different than the other sixty-year-old, white, male colleagues I had grown up with in the profession, a diamond in the rough, authentic and true to himself in a gruff, trustworthy way. Our partnership agreement was a step above

121

a handshake. I aspired to equal partnership and thought I had found it here with him. During the first years of getting established, my investment in the firm was more about the promise of a future than immediate financial security. We still had my husband's income in addition to my negligible paycheck. It didn't matter that my new partner's way was different than mine and that he didn't need the income from the business the same way I did.

I was ambivalent about the role of my own masculine energy, its agency in my success. I needed its steadfast nature and supportive presence to work for me in a positive way. But I resisted it like I resisted time. Time was money. I was good at deadlines. I knew I was a good architect, a valuable member of any team, responsible to a fault. That was what seemed most important, even after becoming a mother and reckoning with the altered view of life that came with being a mother of a child with special needs. Being responsible for children in a consistent, nurturing way required letting go of time. My developing ability to make space for things to develop organically, in life and in quiltmaking, had begun to enter into my professional process. But even though I enjoyed empowering the teams I was a part of and watching how positive change could occur naturally during construction, it still wasn't without the stress that came with feeling responsible for associated cost increases, for which most clients never seemed prepared.

When my marriage began to fail and divorce was on the table, I knew I had to be involved in the business differently. I had to make a living and support my family as a single mother. I couldn't keep putting all our company income back into the partnership with the hope that someday I might be able to pay myself too. I had to rely even more consciously on the energy of my own masculinity for support in all areas of my life now, and I had to make clear choices that could serve me and my children first. I was vulnerable. I felt the need to protect.

I was still sewing in the wee hours of the morning at the dining room table while everyone slept. With fifty completed blocks to work with, it was time to assemble them into a quilt design. The fabrics I had chosen were mostly bright and patterned, and even though I tried to provide some balance with solid colors, the overall effect of all these blocks together felt overwhelmingly bold. I played with different configurations on the design wall until the order I was watching for emerged. Four of the squares could be put together to form a large block that held an irregular diamond shape. A larger center diamond could be formed within a rectangle defined by ten of these large blocks. They were tacked up on the wall with my characteristic blank spaces in between. Then the magic began. Introducing pieces of unique hand screened fabric with oversized gold and blue donut-like circles initiated a colorful blending of energies. The contrast between the soft circles and the bold squares became another kind of pairing, another opportunity for masculine and feminine to come together. I could always feel the flow that took over when this next level of design happened. There were no words at this point. Just the art. It became a very large quilt, as I knew it would. It filled every inch of my design wall. In my small studio space, I had to stand with my back plastered to the opposite wall to take it all in and see the uniquely formed diamonds emerging. There was strength in the sashing that bound and highlighted at the same time. The diamonds felt authentic in their raw shape, bold and masculine. The flow happening in the gaps between felt deep, yielding, and feminine. Both energies were absolutely necessary for the balance of the design.

Recognizing the diamonds in the rough here evoked a quality of masculinity that I admired. I grew up with strong handsome men; my father and brother were both athletes and leaders in their walk through life, each exuding the kind of authentic maleness to which women gravitate. It didn't matter that I couldn't remember ever seeing either one of them shed tears. I felt their vulnerability and accepted their different way of expressing passion and sensitivity. I knew they both loved me and would protect me. I celebrated the quality of masculinity I shared with them, which made me passionately decisive and action oriented, too. But I also felt marginalized by the masculinity of my appearance. I looked like them. All through high school I never believed I could be beautiful with my dark skin, dark hair, and dark eyes. I didn't embody my mother's kind of beauty, the blond hair and light eyes that the men in my family seemed attracted to, that fashion magazines seemed to glamorize. But the beauty I needed to feel could flow through my hands when I made things. The feminine me could be fully present with the masculine me while I was in the throes of creative process.

The sparkling maleness I gravitated to in my husband came with an aroma of authenticity that was impossible to ignore. The smell of him was intoxicating to me. Pheromones, surely, but it always felt like something deeper and more primal. By the time I met him I was old enough to recognize the diamond-in-the-rough quality that set him apart from other men. In addition to his compelling aroma, he was creative and sensitive and passionate about me. I wanted to touch that softer aspect of masculinity in the worst way. It didn't take long to fall in love and to know that he would be the father of my children.

My husband was also an architect. When we met, I was just the intern in the NYC office where he was the project architect for a big new building. It was the year between college and graduate school. I was twenty-two and he was thirty-two. We flirted; the scent of him was doing its work even then. But nothing came of it. He took me out to dinner the night before I left for Boston and it felt like a final goodbye. I thought I'd never hear from him again. But after a few months in my new graduate school life, the letters began to arrive. Wonderfully witty and surprisingly heartfelt letters. I received a package from him at school one day containing a T-shirt with the Superman logo screened on front. Embedded in the big red S was the word *Architect.* It was soft and well-worn with small frays at the neck edge. When I brought it up to my face and inhaled, it smelled like him. He believed in me, and he offered support in the way only he could, encouraging me to continue becoming a Superwoman architect.

My internship that year took place in an office with two male partners and a staff of male architects of all ages and experience—with the exception of one woman, who sat in the back corner of the office. She would leave as needed to take care of her children. My only experience with female leadership in the profession was the office I worked in following graduate school. It was an unprecedented partnership of one man and two women. Both women were married but neither had children. I took note, but the significance of this didn't really sink in. Now, at forty-seven, I was far enough into my career as a business owner to be a role model for younger women entering the profession. I had recently met with one such woman over lunch, sharing with her my story of the year after Ben was born, when I gave up my small, growing architecture practice and my erratic income to work for a regular paycheck with a larger firm. The job was a good fit in many ways, and I enjoyed the work. But I'd had a taste of leading my own charge, and I inquired right away about the track for partnership. At the time, all three principal partners and all the associates were men. They were appreciative enough of my contribution to the firm, but it took only a few more months for me to realize that I would never be honored with acceptance into this particular club. Along with the realization came a shocking question. Were these sixty-year-old white men, who had chosen architecture as a way to express their creativity, jealous of my ability to perform the ultimate creative act? Only women could grow and birth a baby. Designing a building was metaphorically similar, after all; it had been likened to growing and birthing, even with a similar average time frame of nine months (so documented in a Renaissance treatise on architecture I had read).

It took many years and relationships with many different kinds of men, both personally and professionally, before I considered what it might mean to be an equal partner in relationship. *Did men also yearn for equal partnership?*

When I posed this question to my young lunch companion, the one who had come to me in search of mentorship, I saw the look of shock on her face. What was I thinking, sharing this with her? I felt her withdraw immediately behind the same wall of fear and distrust that I had built for myself so many years ago when I was her age. This was the kind of knowing that I had guarded and protected in myself after years of experiencing what felt like callous dismissal by beloved men in my life. *You are too emotional. You are too sensitive. You have no common sense.* And, most confusing, *You are an Amazon woman.* My intuitive knowledge was not scientific. It was something to fear. Thousands of women were burned at the stake centuries ago for this very reason. If the men didn't believe me, then how could I trust my own knowing?

Then there was my cousin Curtis. My relationship with him was one of the few places where I felt safe enough to let the intuitive me be fully present with a man. We were born within two weeks of each other. Family photo albums document a history of being held together, crawling together, playing together, and sharing family events together. He died of Aids the day of Ben's first birthday. We were just thirty-six years old. Curtis had been one of the sparkling diamonds of male companionship in my life. He was handsome and charismatic, creative and full of charitable energy. He made it clear early on that he would always be there for me in the way only certain men could be. He trusted me. He announced his homosexuality silently by simply taking me to his favorite gay bar in town and introducing me to his friends. He stood up for me at my wedding beside my brother and the best man. He was living in Philadelphia with his partner, as he did until the very end, still operating the small restaurant they had successfully created. I took the kids there to visit with him one last time the summer before he passed. He was almost blind at this point, but still managed to teach three-year-old Molly to make croissants in his beloved kitchen. He held and played with Ben, openly passing on his hard-won wisdom there, too. For me he had been the most beautiful example of male and female energy blending, fully expressed and joyfully lived. He, too, held a prominent place in this quilt.

Shortly after completion, *Diamonds in the Rough* was hung in a group show I participated in with three other women quilters. It would be the first time I could see all my work together in one place. My artist statement for the show said, *I come to quilt-making as an architect, interested in the tension between what can be planned and what can be seen or discovered as a basis for design.* One evening before the opening, I felt prompted to ask my daughter, "Of all the things I do in addition to being your mother—architecture, energy medicine, quilting, and community service—what do you think of first when you think of me?" She didn't hesitate for even a second; the word *quilting* was out of her mouth before I could take another breath. I was shocked to hear what I had been hoping for. It wasn't until I was walking through the display of my quilts with a dear friend that I saw how my identity as a woman who embraced her feminine qualities in an obvious way as a quiltmaker might be able to coexist with my identity as a woman who embraced her masculine qualities as an architect. She stopped in the middle of the display, looked at me and said, "*THIS* is who you are."

The architecture partnership that had brought me to Amherst ended in 2012. As much as I valued being part of something bigger than me, I knew it was time to create a context for work that could embrace and honor my feminine way of letting the unknown be part of the design process.

It was the year Ben began college and moved into a dorm. He was home one weekend from school when I casually asked him if he'd like a new quilt for his bed. I received an enthusiastic *Yes!* I asked him if he had a favorite color he'd like me to use, and without hesitation he said, *Pink! I want pink!* I was a bit taken aback at my own response. Outwardly I smiled, but inside I was rebelling at his choice. Men didn't wear pink. I shared my dilemma with his sister Molly and she just laughed, teasing, "Since when are colors so gender identified for you, Mom?" So I paused and gave some space to the idea that Ben's quilt could be pink, or at least feel pink. Before I took him back to school that weekend, I asked him to pick out ten pieces of fabric from my stash, anything at all. The selection was not all overtly pink, but enough to carry pink energy. I found the leftover companion patchwork blocks made years ago, put them up on my design wall, and began to play. Within a week, I had constructed a top using Ben's fabric choices cut into large triangles to fill the spaces between blocks. I added a border, assembled the sandwich with batting and backing, and had everything basted together ready for quilting in just a few days' time.

I didn't quite finish the hand quilting on Ben's quilt for Christmas, but wrapped it up and gave it to him anyway. He had been watching

Ben's quilt, 2012

me stitch for the past few weeks since coming home for the holidays, and he was thrilled to discover that I had been making this quilt for him. I spent the rest of the holiday break finishing it—hours and hours of stitching it all together while feeling the significance of Ben's brilliant presence in the house again. He had become the most accessible embodiment of the diamond-in-the-rough quality of male energy I loved to be around. And for Ben, there was no hiding the softer, vulnerable aspects of his being. His heart was an open book. What an incredible amount of courage and strength it must take for him to function all day long with that feeling. He had grown into a beautiful man with an athletic physique that he put to good use playing soccer and basketball, swimming, kayaking, and especially dancing. He was completely comfortable in his body. He could evoke joy in another person just by moving to the beat of his own drum.

Yet even with Ben, there was some karmic pull to tears that would leave him fighting for control. I would find him alone in his room with a look of despair on his face that seemed so contrary to his usual cheery way. I would ask, even cajole, *what is it Ben, why are you so sad?* and his face would crumple, his body would collapse, and he would let go of heart-wrenching sobs. There was always an unearthly quality to his anguish. My fierce love held him tight during these times as I thought, *if he can do this, then so can I.* When it was over, it was over. There was never any clear explanation. I didn't try to figure it out. Ben was a gift. I imagined he must be channeling something primal and essential for the health of men throughout time.

I can still only see the balance and blending of masculine and feminine energies in *Diamonds in the Rough* from a distance—testimony to the perspective necessary for discerning an essential truth. ❧

Reverie

There's always a story on the surface that we use to defend ourselves, isn't there? Then there's another story, the true story, right behind it. I see the story that weaves the loss of my innocence into every moment I have felt joy and believed I didn't deserve to feel it. I keep feeling joy anyway and so there is confusion. All these years of confusion. I have only fleeting experiences with knowing that I don't have to suffer.

I wake from dreaming to hear Mommy, can I come home now? resonating in my heart.

Is it possible that I am already there?

Another Story # 3, 2004

11

Another Story

I had an idea for a series of quilts, which I began to work on in 2004. I had just learned the technique of reverse appliqué, a process that enticed me with the same kind of magic I had felt playing with scratch boards as a kid. With a sharp point, we could cut out a design or picture from the surface on top to discover that there is some other color, design, or picture underneath. With each emerging detail, the story or picture on top could be transformed by the detail of the order emerging from below.

Another Story #1, 2003

It's like what happens when you tell someone the gist of a story in abbreviated form, but one of the details triggers a memory of something hidden and we say, *But that's another story!* And quickly move on without actually telling *that* story. What stays on top is appropriate, immediate, accessible, conscious, light.

Another Story #2, 2004

What stays hidden for another time is full of promise, unconscious, dark, scary, still alive. I wanted to explore the meaning that could emerge while working with these aspects of light and shadow. What came to mind were the bars of light I saw one night coming out of a dream. They were floating down around me like gentle rain. The widths

133

of the rectangular bars remained constant while the varying lengths moved around each other evoking the feeling of a piece of music from another world.

It was easy to transcribe this feeling to a piece of paper in two dimensions as a simple abstract drawing. I made some basic decisions about scale for the first quilt and began to consider fabric. I had just received a gift of beautiful Japanese fabric squares that Kathy had sent me from Australia. I had also just acquired a unique piece of hand-dyed

cloth made by a colleague. There was a huge contrast between these two fabrics; one could even say they clashed. I became excited about the possibility of creating balance by revealing another story behind the surface pairing of these two opposites. The technique of reverse appliqué was perfect for creating context that could support the revelation of something new.

I decided to work in series with this idea: getting out of the way what you need to get out of the way to get to what you really want to communicate.

I dove into the first quilt while negotiating a marriage that was completely stuck. My husband and I were both hiding the disappointment that had been building over the years. We were each operating with individual coping mechanisms that did not create common ground or a place for mutual support. With no movement happening in either direction—toward renewed commitment and growth, or toward separation and divorce—I was aching for something to give.

I don't think it's a coincidence that this was also the year my grand-mother came to live with us for a brief time before moving to an assisted living facility just down the road. Getting Gramma settled in her new apartment involved hanging her mother's portrait in a prominent place. As I was doing this, she sat quietly watching, as if re-living the fantastic story she loved to tell, one I had been hearing versions of my whole life. It went something like this:

Born in Eastport, Maine in 1887, Kathleen Elinor Apt (nicknamed Cassie) was the fifth of ten children. Her father, Daniel Apt, moved the family to Portland when Cassie was just a child and established himself as a successful sea captain. The Apt family lived a life of affluence and prestige in the bustling growing Portland community. Cassie was de-veloping into a real beauty and was courted by many. With this came rules of etiquette and social responsibility that taxed her generous and independent spirit. She discovered she could escape the pressure of her prescribed future and spread her wings by exploring every inch of her beloved Maine Coast. Eventually, this exploration extended down into Massachusetts and the bustling city of Boston where she would visit her Aunt Grace. Just nineteen years old in 1907, she would secretly and silently walk the streets of this historic city, innocently unaware of her beauty and of the fate that awaited her in Charlestown.

The Schrafft Candy Co. was located in Charlestown and had a suc-cessful presence in Boston during the thriving first decade of the twen-tieth century. By 1907, it was famous not only for its candy but also for the beautifully crafted boxes that the candy came in, made of metal with hand painted images of everything from flowers to beautiful women to scenes of modern life. An artist named Baron was employed as one of the candy box painters. It is not known how or when Cassie was chosen to model for a series of paintings for Schrafft's. What is known is that Cassie and Baron fell in love with each other while he painted her portrait to place on the lid of a distinctive box.

It was forbidden love for each of them.

Baron had arrived in the United States as a young man, after traveling to countries all over the world as a shipmate. It began when he was eight years old; he fled his abusive father in Gothenburg, Sweden, and becoming a stowaway on a ship leaving port. He learned to speak five languages, became an accomplished musician and artist, and was reunited with his brother Richard when he arrived in Boston.

Details are vague as to how others of Baron's family emigrated to the United States, and little is known of them except that they belonged to the Swedish Lutheran religion and only married fellow Lutherans. Baron was promptly disowned by what little family he had here for choosing a life with his beloved non-Lutheran Cassie. Cassie's staunch New England family regarded the Swedish artist as beneath their position in Portland society. She, too, was cut off from her family as a result of choosing a life with Baron.

There's a gap in the story at this point, as there is no record of their marriage or where exactly they established their new life together in Boston. There is only a whisper of whatever scandal made them pack up with their baby boy, Baron Jr., and leave town during the night, never to return. They lived like gypsies travelling the country for years, during which time their first daughter, Virginia, was born. They eventually settled in Rochester, New York. It was the during the Depression and life was hard. They had six children together and Baron managed to make a meager living primarily as a muralist for theaters. He was an angry man. Cassie never complained about his bad humor, or what she gave up to be his wife and mother to their children. She worked tirelessly as a laundress to help supplement the family income and devoted herself to the family. She was known for her tolerance and kindness, and through all her disappointments, Cassie loved and honored Baron.

Gramma would tell this story every chance she could. It was as if she was keeping alive an image from her childhood that projected the safety of a family love that she needed to believe in. I grew up not only with this story but also with the image of my great-grandmother Kathleen as she appeared in the painted portrait that always lived in Gramma's home over the fireplace. My fantasy was that my great-grandfather, Baron, was the artist who painted this portrait. Never speaking the assumption out loud or being told otherwise, this became truth for me. Only when I was well into my thirties did I learn that my grandmother had commissioned this portrait to be made from a photograph she had of her mother. Even then, I continued to romanticize this portrait. Underneath the auburn hair swept up into a loose chignon on top of her head, there was the demure and captivating smile. Her eyes were downcast and hidden from view. It was the face of a woman with a secret. It suggested seduction, an intimate feeling of knowing without really knowing. I imagined that this must be what my great-grandfather experienced when he was painting her. I had also internalized the feeling of unconditional love Kathleen had for her Baron. Year after year Gramma would tell this love story of her parents. It felt significant. Named after my great-grandmother Kathleen, I took the lineage seriously. After all, I too had fallen in love with an artist and was experiencing hardship. I too was devoted to family, determined never to leave, no matter what. I realized that Gramma's own life had followed a path to this truth. Her love story included meeting my grandfather at eighteen years old, a gorgeous man nicknamed Mac who was crazy in love with her and called her 'Spook'. My mother was born nine months later. They had a tumultuous relationship which ended with his death when my mother was only sixteen. But growing up, I never once heard Gramma talk about loving Mac. I learned about their volatile love affair from the bits and pieces that emerged from my mother sharing her own story. By all accounts he was a beloved member of the family, generous, kind and devoted to his Spook. I can still feel the warmth of her hand stroking my back as I lay with my head in her lap, together on the porch of my childhood home as she told me that this had once been the home she shared with Mac, too. I was only four years old. What did I know of secrets then?

I can also still feel the warm sensation in the pit of my belly that I felt while sitting in the historic Quincy Market bar with the man who would be my husband. It was just a year after I finished graduate school. He lived in New York City and we had been carrying on a commuter romance between Boston and New York for the previous six months, five months and two weeks longer than the time it took for me to know I wanted to marry him.

It was a crisp fall day and we had just had a fun walk about town, holding hands and appreciating the beauty surrounding us. We were lovers three generations after my great-grandparents, also finding our story in the streets of Boston. Sipping beers, we fell into easy conversation. Since marriage wasn't openly on the table yet, the conversation took on the quality of a dream, carrying the unspoken energy of a possible life together. I was ready to set the world on fire with my passion for architecture. He wasn't passionate about the profession the way I was. His passion was painting, and now apparently, me. He was living the life of an artist in a loft in NYC and creating huge canvases that exploded with color and mastery of form. As we sat there ruminating about life, I felt the question rise up in me and find voice before I could think about it. I simply asked, "What do you want?" With clarity and dignity he replied, "I will always want to paint."

That's when I fell in love with him. I fell in love with the promise of the artist and his awareness of his truth. I fell in love with his dream. This dream held my heart in a love story where I would support him in his truth while playing out my role as the successful professional that I believed myself to be.

I had my story and I was sticking to it.

I bought the love story, sensing, maybe even knowing, that there was another story—one shaped by beliefs born of fear of exposure, scandal, passion or forbidden love. The romanticized story on the surface guided the choices I made on a day-to-day basis for comfort and success, while the edgier, more human and heartfelt story remained hidden in the shadows of unacknowledged truth. I bought the romanticized version perhaps because it was part of an energetic pattern that had been passed down through generations. Was my place in the family lineage the result of unresolved issues from another life and the choice to reincarnate a way to keep working on lessons I needed to learn? Or was the story the result of unresolved trauma and grief from early childhood wounding? With enough time gone by, I could realize that life was not a romance novel; eventually, each version of the story held truth.

My grandmother Virginia was the second oldest of Cassie & Baron's six children. She never believed she was beautiful as she believed her mother to be, often telling me she thought she had a nose like a witch. But I look at the photos of her as a teenager and know what Mac saw as beautiful. There was the wild spirit, barely contained, that lit up her beautiful blue eyes, her mane of blond hair befitting the big-hearted young lioness that she was. She was an adventurer who had been taught that responsibility to family came first. She became a businesswoman as soon as she could convince someone she was old enough and went on to have a successful career in real estate. But the struggle to be a responsible daughter, partner, and mother at the same time broke something in her. She drank too much, drove expensive cars too fast, had horses and furs while her daughter had to pay for her own college. She was manipulative, and at the same time charming with everyone she met. Her driving need to be successful was in direct contrast to the gentle spirit of my grandfather who just wanted her to be happy, and as the story goes, anytime he tried to say no to her or go his own way, she would begin to roar. When I was seventeen, my brother and I were having a professional photo taken of us together to give to our parents for their anniversary. I asked Gramma if I could borrow her car in order to keep the appointment a secret. She said sure, but only if I gave her a copy of the photo. Without hesitating I said *no*, explaining that this was a special gift just for Mom and Dad. Her response was to sit down at our dining room table and start crying. She just wasn't used to being denied what she wanted.

Of course, this is just my version of her story.

If I had to write a script for *Another Story #1* it would be something like this: *It is time to get married. Fall in love. Choose a pairing of two contrasting and very different individuals to make a life together. Weave a love story to support this union. Make an attempt at balance by creating family and introducing children into the design. Put in the time and the effort. Create a legacy of stitched, quilted lines of shared history in a further attempt to bring the design into balance. Recognize that something has to change.*

It's hard to find the reset button when you are in the center of living the story you've written. I struggled with this quilt. I was following my own set of rules but couldn't feel my heart in the work. I needed the process to lead me to what I needed to see and accept that I might not like what was there. I was terrified of looking at the possibility that my husband hadn't really wanted to get married at all. I tell the story of his proposal, joking that it was like something out of a Woody Allen movie, quirky and romantic. *Come to New York and move in with me*, he says, to which I replied defiantly, *If I come back to live in New York, I'll be moving in with Kathy!* To which he replies, *Screw Kathy, come back to New York and marry me!* To which I begin to cry. It is only after he emphatically says that he is serious and wants an answer that I say *yes*.

Working on *Another Story #1*, I began to recognize that I could experience the thrill of exposing something I was feeling but didn't know how to express; I could make a choice about what to keep or change about this feeling right then and there. It was just fabric and thread, after all. I could fleetingly experience whatever shame or fear or disappointment I was feeling about my role in our crumbling marriage and let it remain intentionally exposed instead of hiding it again. Alternatively, I could change something to make the design prettier, more palatable, or simply bearable. I didn't feel entirely comfortable or safe with what was emerging, but I managed to stay with the process. It was enough for the moment.

The bars of light in my dream became the brightly colored odd pieces of fabric in this quilt, introduced in the cut-out spaces of reverse appliqué. They were almost jarring at first, chosen for their shock value, but they could integrate and harmonize. At first I was committed to letting them be what they were, instead of changing anything for the sake of a more harmonious appearance. I could feel the rightness of this non-action and how it stirred things up to keep the angst I was feeling on the surface. Staying there, I decided to machine quilt the piece by methodically outlining and extending the linear patterns in the hand dyed fabric. There was a certain satisfaction in defying each soft line by extending it from edge to edge of the quilt as if it needed to define something or lead somewhere. What resulted was the feel of intellectually inspired hard edges, of precision, a maze of double lines describing a vain attempt to impose order in the design. I still couldn't find the heartbeat of this piece. So I made a final attempt at softening. I appliquéd complementary gray pieces back in between the double quilt-

Another Story, #1, detail

ing lines to cover up portions of the bright contrasts.

Like a patch on a wound, this helped to tone down the pain that still had no clear path for release. These pieces enabled the pain to integrate and connect with otherwise disparate elements across the quilt. With these tenuous but clear bridges in place, I could let go and move on to the next quilt in the series. Meanwhile, Gramma was slipping into a new landscape in her mind. Our outings together and visits to the house were less and less frequent as she continued to retreat. It was a revelation to me that she was forgetting her limiting stories and in the space that opened up in her, she was finding her heart.

For *Another Story 2,* I chose softer fabrics and softer contrasts finished with softer hand quilted lines. A palette of turquoise, muted oranges and shades of purple became the backdrop for the bars of floral fabric to express themselves. The composition formed quickly on the design board. I wasn't thinking about construction technique or how I would piece it all together. There was no clear script guiding the

Another Story, #2, detail

process this time. I was simply being led by the love I was experiencing. I was in love with the light offered to me through the assemblage of these seemingly random pieces of fabric in such an unexpected way, with the feel of the soft rich orange and purple wools that punctuated and created depth. I loved how one piece of designer fabric could yield so many variations of plum and rust in patterns that reached through the whole quilt. I loved the entire network of quilted curves that emerged from simple leaf patterns.

I loved every minute of every hour spent in this space, effortlessly feeling connection. The softness that emerged in the making of the piece enveloped me and I felt my femininity like a cloak of much-needed mother love. With resolve to stay here, I took my time and spent months completing the work. The story of architect-wife was transforming into one of female artist finding her voice. I was feeling my vulnerability now. And after years of keeping my path as a healer hidden from even my own awareness, I could finally settle into this vulnerability and follow where my heart was leading.

My decision to enroll in a four-year energy medicine training in 2005 was the moment my husband said that the marriage was over, Training required time and money and support that I knew I would never receive from him. I intuitively knew that I was beginning to rewrite my story, and with the same kind of self-awareness he demonstrated during our courtship, and he knew that he didn't want to be part of this new story. I was a partner in my own architecture firm with the flexibility and resources to be able to make this commitment. He knew he couldn't stop me from entering new territory just because he didn't want me to go there. At the nursing home, I would share my excitement about embarking on this new path with Gramma. She would just smile, pat my hand and say, *That's nice dear.* Then, holding hands, we would take our ritual stroll around the corridors while family members of fellow residents would stop to say hi to Gramma and then tell me that of all the residents there, she was their favorite. We would walk silently and I would wonder if the reason Mac called her Spook was because she, too, *knew things* and *had sensitivities.* I would wonder at the connection between us that was becoming stronger and stronger the less we used words. She, and the world she now lived in, had become a clear source of support for me as I moved forward.

Another Story 3 was made in the first year of my training. It was the year that the proverbial dam burst and all the ways I had been holding myself back in the marriage and in life were illuminated. First-year work was focused on bringing hidden issues to the surface to be seen and eventually healed. We learned hands-on healing techniques that could help loosen the energetic grip on these hidden wounds that resulted in suffering, illness, and, ultimately, projection onto loved ones.

I began the quilt by making blocks of recombined strips from a single piece of fabric, and discovered that using a striped or linear patterned fabric yielded the most interesting results. What was once linear and one-dimensional now had a dynamic and multi-dimensional quality. This multi-dimensional quality appeared most clearly when adjacent to a solid color, so that each block could became a gem with adequate space around it to be truly seen.

I had formed a deep bond with one of my teachers in the training. I knew I was experiencing love in way I never had before and it was confusing. This triggered a whole new set of questions about the relationship between commitment and unconditional love. The combinations of reds and blues in the quilt became a metaphor for both my passion and my voice eventually finding clear expression through the confusion. But having dark-night-of-the-soul panic for days at a time, as I negotiated a new way of experiencing love that I didn't understand, was terrifying. The solid black paths that were revealed through reverse appliqué became both the necessary structure and the scary unknown paths in front of me. I lovingly hand embroidered each edge of these paths with a strong blanket stitch, as if to acknowledge the enduring quality of the unknown.

It would take many more years to work through all the shadow issues hidden in these paths. Even in the certainty that what was happening to me was independent of the love I still felt for my husband, I could no longer ignore the state of the marriage and the accompanying disappointment of a failing partnership. I was learning most poignantly that my husband was not the bad guy here. All we had to do was mutually agree to revise the terms of the unwritten contract we had made with each other before having children. I knew I needed to keep growing and he knew he needed for everything to stay exactly the way it was. We simply couldn't find the mutual middle ground and eventually, we lost

Another Story, #3, detail

the way to a place where we could fight for the marriage.

So far, the quilts in this series had kept to variations on a theme in a recognizable way. My love story with my husband had been true, until it wasn't true anymore. What began as gray and rigid and confused at the beginning had transformed into a clear expression of a voice and a path. My heart was broken open in the process and a journey with healing found solid ground.

It was the beginning of a new story.

The fourth and final quilt of this series, *Another Story 4,* became a transformation of the theme. It allowed me to reflect on and celebrate where I was right then in the bold curves of bright red outrage *and* passion, joy *and* sadness, not fully liberated *and* no longer in denial. It had been four years since I began this series. The story of my failing marriage was coexisting with the story of my breaking free from illusion. I continued to follow the process established in *Another Story 3* by making blocks from a small set of random fabrics. They were strip-pieced using free-form, spontaneous curves, cut again, and recombined. The curve of sensuous red wool became both the leading edge and the anchor of each of the resultant gems. As I quilted along these edges, I realized that the energy of these curved paths would always come back to begin with me. And at each return, I could choose another story.

It wasn't until after my grandmother's passing in 2011 that I saw a copy of the photo that the now-legendary portrait of Cassie was made from. With shock, I realized that great liberties had been taken in the translation of the stark black-and-white picture. The heavier, more serious expression on my great-grandmother's face had become the colorful portrait of seductive promise in the painting. How did this happen? I was fascinated with how my grandmother, in her own romanticized memories of her mother, had guided the process of this portrait to result in an image that was *her* truth. I couldn't help but wonder now what liberties she had taken with her parents' love story. I would never know the truth. All I had was the experience of hearing her story, where I went with it, how it moved through me and became something else. ❋

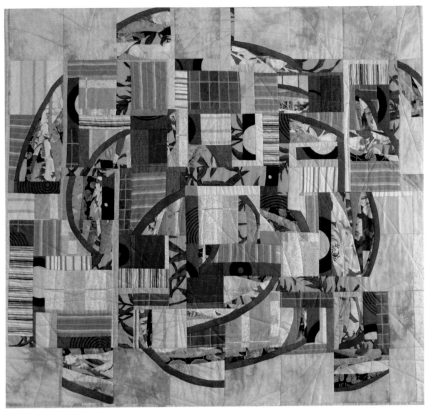

Another Story # 4, 2006

Reverie

Ah, the drama that forms on the roller coaster of loving so deeply one moment, only to feel such devastating disappointment over and over again in the fall. I want to finally stop riding the roller coaster and give my spirit a rest from the ravages of an ego that needs to be right about love. The bridge I am crossing and need to burn is the deep disappointment I feel when a heart closes to my love. I want to get off the roller coaster and instead be the little girl on the swing who has stopped being afraid of the make-believe demons who control my journey of love.

Many Moons, panel 3

12

Many Moons

The making of *Many Moons* was a year-and-a-half long endeavor that began the day I sat with Margaret in the spring of 2008, waiting for our kids to finish their swim practice. We knew each other best as yogi friends participating in a local 'Yoga Sutra' discussion group together. But instead of diving into a conversation about the path to enlightenment that day, we were discussing the best places to buy fabric. Sitting at the edge of the pool with the background music of rhythmic slap and splash, I shared about my recent quilting work, and she shared about recent sewing projects she was enjoying with her daughter. She asked about seeing my quilts, saying she had an oddly shaped wall in her kitchen great room that she was reserving for fabric art: *maybe you have something?* There was no pause, no thinking this over; she simply followed me home right after practice to look at what I had to offer. I laid all my finished pieces out on the floor of my small home studio.

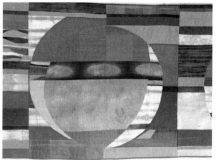

Top, Many Moons, panel 1
Below, Many Moons, panel 2

On her knees, she flipped through the stack of finished quilts like pages of a book, expressing her delight with oohs and ahhs, stopping at a few she really liked, disappointed that they were the wrong size for her wall. Eventually, she looked up with the expression of one ready to make a commitment and asked, "Do you do commission work?" Me smiling, "Of course." That settled it. I went to her house the next day, measured the wall the quilt would be living on, and began to dream.

One of the many extraordinary aspects of making this piece on commission was the way Margaret engaged with the process. I had picked a palette of color and fabric that I knew resonated for her. But beyond that, she felt no need to be involved. When I asked if she wanted to review some sketches I had made for a conceptual design she said, "No, I trust that what you make will be exactly right. "I had permission to follow the energy of what was developing without conditions, without an agenda. And whereas I was growing used to this in my own process and work, it was the first time that I had consciously experienced such unconditional trust from another and the creative freedom that can result.

It would be months before I actually began making something. Margaret was in no hurry, and I was waiting for inspiration. It finally came with a series of photographs taken at Cape Cod while walking the beach during low tide on the bay side, where the retreating water would leave evocative patterns in a vast expanse of sand. I was a year divorced. I had just finished the third year of my energy medicine training. I was in love. I knew that much. But there was nothing clear about the feeling. I couldn't grasp what honestly expressed love looked or felt like. I was living with this emotion from inside a tightly wound ball that had begun to unravel. I couldn't dare focus on the possibility that I might be in love with my teacher, Richard, and that it might have been this love that finally broke my marriage beyond repair. I drifted along those broad stretches alone after each low tide, feeling the grief that seemed to be with me all the time now. I was mesmerized by the beautiful grooves that would pull me along and then suddenly morph into something else as another stream merged with it. I was in love with the episodic quality of water meeting sand. I would follow a specific combination of shadow and water in each rivulet with my eyes, while feeling the silky texture of the tender ridges collapse under my footsteps. This vast terrain was so exposed in the retreating tide, so vulnerable to the slightest intervention. How could I not pay attention to what was shifting inside of me too?

My connection to Richard existed within the firm boundaries of a teacher-student relationship. Famous throughout the school for his hugs, he would simply open his arms and wait for you to enter his enormous energetic field. His large arms would enfold ever so gently but firmly and here he would stay for what seemed like a very long time. It was impossible not to sigh and settle into trust in one of his hugs. At the end of a class weekend during the first year of our training, I waited to be the last to say goodbye to him, wanting one of his famous hugs in the worst way. Open and vulnerable from the transformative work of the weekend, I would be returning home to a husband who was resentful of the process I had chosen to engage in, and two children who sensed the shifts occurring in their mother, but had no clear understanding why. It would be years before I understood that the intimacy of this work that felt so intermittently captivating could be something constant and normal. In the meantime, I needed the validation of physical heart-to-heart with another human being.

Standing there that night in a hug with Richard, something light and timeless opened in me. I heard sobs even in the absence of tears. Deep resonant sobs that infused every molecule of the space I seemed to be suspended in. Were they my sobs or Richard's? Maybe universal collective sobs? I would never know. The hug ended. We said goodnight; the outside face of this simple, ritual exchange as two people parted seemed ordinary and typical. But for me, everything changed in that moment. The trajectory of whatever path I had been on up to that moment veered off in a very different direction. I was sure that what I had experienced was some kind of love. Not like any kind of love I thought I knew. This love had the terrifying power to catapult me completely and irrevocably into unknown territory. And even though I knew Richard was just being my teacher, I couldn't extricate myself from the man. I drove home dazzled by the reel that had begun running in my head, flashing through every love I thought I had experienced with every man I thought was *the one*. It was then that I remembered the dream I had about *the fat man in the water that I am in love with*. I realized Richard was the image of the man in the dream. I drove the highway in a kind of numbness I could only feel if I had been caught in a lie, except ten times worse because I didn't even know that there had been a lie to be caught in. I had been so sure that that dream was about my husband.

A few months after this experience I read,

Real teachers leave no traces. They're like the wind at night rushing right through you and totally changing you but leaving everything unchanged, even your greatest weaknesses; blowing away every idea of what you thought you were and leaving you as you always have been, since the beginning. (Peter Kingsley, The Dark Places of Wisdom)

Teacher aside, I was lost to a torrent of emotion. I surrendered. The only thing I could do was strap myself in and go along for the ride. Months of anguished sleeplessness followed. It was a poignant time with my husband. He was convinced I was having an affair, and I was terrified of the affair of the heart I knew I was engaged in. I didn't know how to tell him about my experience with Richard without shattering the illusion of love that was still tethering me to my marriage. That tether finally snapped one night when he found me huddled in a corner of the living room couch in the wee hours. He demanded to know what was wrong with me. When I couldn't offer anything coherent beyond, *something is opening in me and I don't know what it is*, he told me, simply and definitively, that he didn't want to go there with me.

The quilt finally began as an exploration of repeating forms left by the retreating waves in sand—undulating lines that could move across the very long stretch of empty wall in Margaret's home. I could see and feel each moment in each ripple of each photograph, a continuum of energy that could easily morph into form. I don't know where the series of spheres came from or exactly when they appeared. It was if the waves opened up on a whim and made space for them to be seen: in sequence, like phases of a single moon, capturing a moment of illumination in the cycle of its orbit; or like many moons, each with the face of a shared story.

I felt very clear about how to proceed. The quilt would be constructed in three sections. I took advantage of my computer graphics skills and the large printer in my office to make templates for each moon. There wasn't any logic or rationale as to why each moon came out the way it did. My eye guided the composition. I chose a varied palette of textures and types of fabric to work with: wools, cottons, hand-dyed and commercial alike, prioritizing the blues and reds that Margaret seemed drawn to. Each of the three moonscapes would be fully composed and quilted before being attached together to form the final ten-foot length.

I spent the better part of six months composing. My tiny studio and design wall couldn't contain the energy of what I was feeling. Each time I came in to work, I had to lay all the pieces out on the floor in sequence anew, to see relationships as they were developing. I would work for a day or two, and then walk away for weeks. I didn't feel rushed. Sometimes I would enter the studio, look at what was developing, move just one piece into a new place, and walk out. Another day I would get caught up in a frenzied feeling, unable to leave until I achieved both a visible and viscerally felt completion of the moonscape I was focused on.

By spring of 2009, the design was complete, hundreds of pieces of fabric pinned together. It was order restored, sections fitting together just the way they were supposed to be. I loved how the moons seemed to emerge from and at the same time merge with the context in which they lived. The number three played out again in the beautiful hand-dyed piece of fabric that occupied and seemed to scroll through the center of the center moon. It was marked by three moons of its own, and they seemed to draw me into some magical meaning or toward some place where I might resist going. I hadn't thought about the dream of the fat man for a while but it came back now, as if to remind me that it still occupied the center of me in a significant way.

I had been rummaging around in my stuff for years looking for the actual documentation of this dream. I remembered this much clearly: *Driving along a country road with my husband and we stop at a small body of water to the right. It is a perfect circle, feels like a pond. There is a large man treading water right in the center of this pond, dark curly hair and wire rimmed glasses. I can only see his head, I know he is very big and Buddha-like, fat. He has the most angelic smile on his face, looking at me. I enter the water to his right and he turns to face me as I swim gently toward him, feeling his smile as I approach. Just as I reach him, I wake up.* Even though I could recall it so clearly, I was sure I had written it detail by intimate detail into one of my diaries. I'd been scouring all my writing back to 1995, desperate for the validation that my memory was true. I even remember telling my mother back then about a series of dreams I was having about "being in love with a fat man" and that I thought this was a metaphor for an unconditional love of my husband, no matter what his physical form.

Looking again through my archives, I found a diary from 1980 that I didn't even know I still had, written when I was twenty-two years old. Just the first few dozen pages had entries, seven of which were written to "Richard." As I read these entries a strange familiarity passed through me. *I feel a peace I have been longing to feel, maintaining and even heightening my energy level and desire to grow, and yet it isn't the frantic longing and anxious questioning that I have always experienced. The peace I feel is one of total understanding, of the spirit. We of the words possess such an infinity of soul that I thought did not exist in this world. . . . I just want to experience the awe of the love I feel.*

I was writing to a Richard of twenty-nine years ago.

I was on fire all over again. The way he used to make me feel. Like the obsession with finding the dream about Teacher Richard, I now couldn't let go of the surge of memory that returned with this *lover* Richard of the past. I was an archaeologist who had just discovered a life-changing artifact. I was a dancer, dancing a choreographed dance with an irresistible partner to all the dreaming I had done together with this man. I thought I had been in love then, too.

Whatever had opened in me had stayed open, open to waves of feeling that kept me questioning every love relationship with a man I'd ever had. Finding the diary from so long ago felt like some kind of divine intervention. How had I forgotten about this lover Richard of the past, the one who wrote me love poems and saw me the way I saw myself when I went deep inside? Curious about where he might be now, it took me but a moment to find him through an internet search, and there he was, looking into my soul once again from the photograph in a Wikipedia entry chronicling his life and career. Successful playwright, comedian, artist, writer, father. I was twenty-two years old again, feeling very stylish with my long thick hair flowing out of a Barbra Streisand style cap, the kind she wore in her movie *What's Up Doc.* I had been subdued after a rowdy weekend spent with a college friend, on my way back to New York, waiting for the train to start moving again after its stop in Philadelphia. He was standing in the aisle, handsome with shocking blue eyes and a slightly crooked mouth. He was staring at me across the empty seat, and he politely asked to sit in it. I don't think it was even ten minutes before he had me doubled over in hysterical laughter with a spontaneously inspired Chihuahua routine. He had my heart before we even pulled into NYC. We exchanged numbers on the platform at Penn station. Our love affair took off like a comet, intense and hot. And like a comet, when the short life of the flare couldn't be sustained, the love affair ended abruptly. We were together four months. And then he was gone.

I began the more focused, technically oriented work of sewing everything together. Once all the sections were completed, the feel of the multitude of pieces now committed to each other compelled me to find backing and batting, laboriously baste the three layers of each section in place, and begin thinking about the quilting stitches that would eventually bind the ten-foot length together. With the same kind of determined precision, I looked up lover Richard on Facebook and sent him a message. After twenty-nine years the comet had come back around—or maybe it was a Saturn return of our connection. Either way, once contact was made, we delved right back into sharing about our lives and discovering that we had been having many of the same experiences along a similar spiritual path. After many emails full of shared intimate detail, he offered his belief that the more obstacles we encounter along a spiritual path, the more opportunity we have for personal growth—that we manifest people in our lives to facilitate that growth. He likened this search for our spiritual descendants as "living the tribe."

As self-proclaimed tribe, we engaged in months of correspondence following this remarkable discovery and reconnection. It was now almost a year since I had begun the quilt. My daughter was graduating from high school and would shortly leave home. I was graduating from my energy medicine program and would shortly find myself face-to-face with the question of where and how I could maintain the kind of intimacy of experience I had come to value through my training. All the while I was steadily merging together the faces of the many moons that wanted to be seen in the quilt. Or maybe three faces of the same moon. Each had its own identity, while waves of complementary color and form kept them inextricably linked to each other.

I began to feel the wind like water moving across each surface, changing the texture of the pattern, prompting another view of the face that has always been there. Each face was now a smooth finished surface of precise seams, and I quilted them reverently

Kathy with Many Moons

with undulating, thick machine stitched lines that would eventually interconnect with those of the face next to it. After the three rectangular sections were joined, more wavy quilting lines were added across edges to connect and fix those particular faces in place. Even when the face of lover Richard from the past disappeared again from my life as it did that summer, I knew it would still always be there.

The sum of the many transitions during that summer of 2009 led me to the completion of the quilt, and into the arms of the next Richard. *Partner* Richard. Meeting him when I did felt like perfect timing. He was intense, intelligent, connected to his land, life, and spiritual life in ways that attracted me wholeheartedly. We met through an internet dating service just a few months after I installed the quilt on Margaret's wall. He occupied the center of the now visible thread of spiritual friends named Richard. Whether teacher, lover, or committed companion, *Richard* was a powerful presence. Each entered into a place in the flow of my journey with love just when I was ready. As soulmates, each showed me an aspect of love I had been denying in myself.

Margaret was the best kind of patron. She believed in me and my work even if I didn't. And she was willing to pay for it. The value I placed on the work of the quilt went unquestioned. When I told her that the fee she was paying me would be financing my trip to California to engage in a one-on-one intensive session with one of my teachers there, to continue to explore where this path in front of me was leading, she smiled and showed me the goosebumps on her arm. Our work together was done.

I am grateful to Margaret for her generosity and her intuitive understanding that what was meant to emerge would emerge. It doesn't matter that *Richard* will never hold the same meaning for her that it holds for me. She simply gets to live, every day, with this expression of the many faces of love I discovered in the process of creation. ❁

Many Moons, installed 2009

Reverie

We need each other to heal, to be, to remember how to be with another, how to honor our self in relation to another. I am liberated. I will always feel the depth of this love, if never to reconcile with our present form in this time. Even if it is to be just the memory of a moment, to remind me how alive I can feel, it is and always will be my liberation. It is a shared quest for healing ourselves, helping others heal themselves, helping our families and communities to wake up and know there is another way.

Mandala Serpent, 2011

13

Mandala

I started dating Richard in the late fall of 2009. Within weeks he took me out for a hike in the woods of the mountain he lived on. It quickly became evident to me that I was being tested. He would veer off trail, scamper up steep inclines and then turn, openly assessing, watching for my response. Of course I kept right up. And though I wasn't taking in the beauty of where I was as keenly as the man in front of me, I knew something transformative was happening. He was leading me to a new depth of experience and into a world that felt like home.

I began to yearn for the sacred piece of land he lived on. I loved being in his house surrounded by woods on one side and a vast open view on the other. I loved the life and community he had created for himself on this land. He had a big organic garden and llamas. He made his own raspberry wine, felled his own trees for firewood, and lived simply. We came from similar middle class backgrounds with fathers who were medical professionals. We both made our living in the design and construction industry. We both loved to ski. With so much in common, I could overlook one big difference. While I had been in the heart of marriage and life with children, he had been living a celibate life in an ashram.

In the course of just two dates we fell in love. We managed the hour commute between our two homes. Our relationship blossomed in the winter cocoon of snow and cold that followed. We practiced yoga and meditation together each morning. I learned how to feed the llamas and call to each one by name, becoming familiar with each personality, and how they liked to nestle in the hay and hide from the cold in the shelter Richard had built for them. We noticed that the alpha llama, who was normally the first to emerge for a meal, wouldn't get up from his warm spot for a whole day, not even to eat. Eventually Richard called the vet, who upon examination, determined that the llama had been infected by a meningeal worm and was in the process of becoming paralyzed. With a long cold winter in front of us, Richard knew there was little hope for recovery and within minutes, made the decision to have the llama put down. I was shocked at how quickly this all happened. The vet prepared the large needle, Richard held the llama's head in his lap while I placed my hands on the llama's body at his heart. The injection was made, there was the briefest struggle, and I felt the beating heart stop with a thud. That was it. From the time the vet had arrived, it had been only an hour. Richard shook with sobs. The ground was already too frozen to bury the body, so it was placed behind the shelter, covered with blankets and more snow with the intention of doing a proper burial in the spring.

Burying the llama turned out to be an arduous job. By the time a hole had been dug, the body had thawed. Richard struggled through the job alone, transferring the now flaccid body in the bucket of his tractor loader into the grave, hoping it was buried deep enough. He was visibly distressed when he returned to the house. In the middle of the night he slipped out of bed, got dressed, said quietly, *I have to go to the hospital*, and left. He didn't have a cell phone and I had no way to contact him. I was stunned. He returned a few hours later and said that he thought he had been having a heart attack, that the emotion of the day had been too much for him. He admitted to having a history of heart related issues, and said that he would routinely take himself to the hospital. I tried to be loving and supportive. But hiding his vulnerability had brought up a deep fear in me. It would wake me up in the middle of the night, take me out of bed and onto the couch in front of the fire downstairs. Sometimes Richard would get up and come sit with me, but mostly I would commune with this fear alone. It would insist I stay awake long enough to feel the full effect of a terrified heart. Was this my fear or his fear I was feeling? Each night I would get back into bed with no resolution, and wake to start a fresh day with my new love.

By the summer of 2010 I had become a regular visitor, watching for how his way could become my way. I had just moved the contents of my studio to the loft room above the barn where we slept in the summer months while giving over the house to his seasonal bed and breakfast business. It was from this newly established center of my creative life that I packed a large suitcase full of fabric to take to my annual quilting retreat at QBL that summer. I was looking forward to starting a new series of quilts to honor this sacred place I was becoming part of.

Settled into our first day of class, I gravitated to photos I had taken just the week before: my mother's bowls. I had quite a collection, given her passion for making pottery. Bowls were her favorite, all sizes, shapes, and colors. Each piece had a simple pattern around the edge and a sin-gular, luscious glaze that represented years of playing with color. I came to the stacks on the side-board in my own kitchen for every meal, choosing to eat from heart made bowls rather that the machine made

Mom's bowls

white stock in my cupboards. The photographs captured for me my own passion for finding nourishment aligned with my mother's passion for finding beauty in simplicity.

Like her lump of clay on the wheel waiting for circular motion to guide the form of her bowl, my quilt began with pieces of solid, pure color radiating around a center, then strip-pieced with corresponding pieces of each color—yellow, orange, green and blue—to extend their fields further.

Mandala Bowls, progress detail

I came into this world through the container of love that was mother. It made sense that I would start here, feel the certainty and the power contained in each simple bowl, as I consciously moved forward into this new, sacred love relationship with a man. The quilt formed around this center. Mandala entered the process and began to inspire the flow of energy that wanted to hold my passion for creating a life with Richard. In its simplest definition, mandala represented the universe. The basic form of a square containing a circle created structure for a microcosm of life to exist in an endlessness of time. Each bowl in this quilt could be a container for another aspect of me that I needed to bring to light through my love relationship.

The design carried a clear balance, but in the end, there were moments that couldn't be contained in the order of color and form that was developing. The oddly shaped blue pieces pushing beyond the circle of containment seemed out of place at first, even a little annoying. But I left them, worked with them, let them integrate and work with the composition in what felt like a pleasing way. It was a reminder that not all is what it seems. This anomaly in the order of things carried questions too: *What needed to be expressed? What voice wasn't being heard?*

Richard and I had started spending time in the White Mountains in a grander expression of our mutual love for being with trees and stone and water. I brought my sewing machine to our new home away from home there, set it up on the dining table and began the process of adding machine-quilted curves. The design of this quilt was not going to change. The hand quilted lines added at the edges were a final soft touch of acquiescence to a man I loved but was still feeling unsure of. We both wanted a commitment that could contain the unpredictability of growth in love. But we had different views for how that growth could happen. My daughter, Molly, was having a rough first year of college emotionally, and I watched for how Richard might engage. But he

Mandala Bowls, 2010

didn't. He loved spending time with Ben, but also loved to dream about how he and I would move to the wilds of New Hampshire when Ben was "on his own." I shared with him my vision of us both selling our respective properties, of finding a new country home located midway between our established communities. He didn't get it, my need to have my own life *and* be available to my family. Instead of feeling the freedom that can come from yielding in a commitment, I began to feel the pressure of an agenda being imposed on me.

While working at the nursing home where I spent a semester interning for my energy medicine training, I had learned that the space of intimacy had no room for agenda. I was working with a woman who was going blind. It took several sessions of just talking with her and assessing before she would even agree to a hands-on healing. Up to this point I had worked with many clients and had been able to successfully maintain the required boundary. Maybe it was because she was about my age and I could identify with her sensitivity that made this dynamic different. Or maybe it was that I sensed she was hiding something behind stubborn resistance. I began to do a simple energy balancing with her, my hands hovering lightly over her body. I was only a few minutes into the work when she said *Stop. I can feel your agenda.* I was humbled, realizing that I might have projected my desire for her to respond a certain way to the work we were doing together. Now in my relationship with Richard, I recognized just how disconcerting it felt to be on the other side of an agenda.

I began making *Mandala Serpent* within a week of finishing *Mandala Bowls*. The center of this quilt featured a kantha (a type of embroidery typical of eastern South Asia) stitched image of a serpent I had

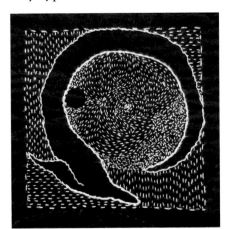

made. A serpent that has shed its skin carried the energy of transformation for me, and in the form portrayed here, in white stitches on black cloth, it was circling back to capture its own tail like an ouroboros (the Greek word meaning "tail devourer"). One of the oldest mystical symbols in the world, the serpent eats its own tail to sustain its own life. From years of practic-

Kantha stitched serpent

ing Continuum, I had come to understand the power of the ouroboros through my own body in response to pleasurable movement. And now, the loop of regeneration and renewal that lived in me was finding new expression in my movement through the forests and mountains with Richard.

Yet no matter how happy I was, or how much pleasure I was experiencing in my adventures with him, the dark side of our relationship was always there. I didn't trust him to fully accept me or my voice. He didn't trust that I could fully commit. As much as he tried to include my children and me as their mother into our relationship, his desire for my undivided attention eventually dominated and would create a large, black space of discord. And then a thrilling display of light would appear to remind me of the strength of our love and its promise of transformation.

I was looking out the upstairs bedroom window, watching while Richard cut sections out of a garden hose with his prize kitchen knife one day. I had no idea what he was doing. My attention was completely riveted on the white-handled knife in his hand. Normally, I could always find this knife on top of the wooden cutting board in the kitchen. I was surprised that he was using it to do a job that could have been done by

any number of tools in his well-stocked wood shop. It had become a challenge for me during my visits, to prepare meals with just this one knife. At first blush, watching the cutting of the garden hose seemed like sacrilege to me. Irresponsible, inconsiderate, and impulsive.

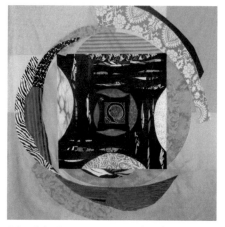

Mandala Serpent, progress detail

But then in an instant it all changed. I was overwhelmed with a feeling of love. I now saw competence, intention, and respect. I felt the focus and satisfaction of his effort, as he stood out there in the expanse of his green lawn fitting the two cleanly severed sections of hose back together. I recognized that he was able to make me, too, the sole focus of his devotion in a single-minded way. Would I be able to make him the focus of my devotion the same way?

I began to encircle the dark center of this quilt and its glimpses of light with broad curves of bright color anchored on a background of green love. I enjoyed the process of watching the circle around the center form. There were many moments when I reveled in the feel of the open, swirling edges of the developing circle.

I resisted urges to leave any part of the circle undefined or broken, and what eventually emerged was a tightly bound container for the center. I decided to hand-quilt the entire piece. Here was an opportunity to practice patience and be present to the beauty, connection, order, and silence that was possible in this relationship. It certainly would give value to the time spent quilting. I was easily distracted. I was constantly brought back to my belief that Richard would never be able to truly honor the mother in me. It was humbling to witness how often I experienced impatience at the desire to feel the relationship differently through all the months it took to finish the quilting.

My husband used to say that time was like a snake coiled around his neck. He meant this in direct relation to me and my obsession with time. I was always on time for appointments. When I wanted to leave at a certain time, I expected everyone to be ready to leave at that time. When I put out a request for something, my idea of a timely response was *right now*, not later. And after becoming a mother, time took on new dimensions. When my baby cried, I couldn't get to her fast enough. When my child had a problem, if time couldn't expand to allow enough space for resolution, then time would be made at the expense of my husband's needs.

My place in the world as *mother* finally found voice during my time with *Mandala Serpent*. Who I was as a mother in relationship with my two children would always come first. It was what defined me and brought me to my balanced center. I couldn't see how this could change, not yet anyway, and I believed that there was no future for my relationship with Richard unless it did. My time with him lasted as long as it took for me to finish the quilt; we separated after a little over a year together. In an effort to stem the flow of heartbreak we were both feeling, we attempted a reconciliation six months later. This time it took only weeks to reach the fateful moment when we faced another separation, and Richard needed to hear me say the words, *I will never want to be in relationship with you ever again.* It felt like there would never be enough time for me to reckon with my fear in this relationship, no matter how much pain the separation caused both of us; hearing these words was the only way he could justify walking away.

Richard's gift was in his holding up a mirror for me to see just how much time conditioned my desire for a relationship to change, to see how lack of trust, masked as impatience, could sabotage a process of growth. In this lifetime, I might get another pass. In the meantime, the process of working with Mandala helped me to settle in the center of where I was with myself, exploring the endlessness of time as much as I could. ❖

Reverie

I am piecing together a quilt in my new mandala series; the unfinished top is now lying flat on my dining room table. I pin the last pieces in place. It is such a satisfying process, turning under the raw edge, resolving how each piece will meet, adjusting an angle here, smoothing out a bulge there, feeling the color adjacencies and fabric choices up close. I go to sit on the couch and I am looking at the whole top from an oblique angle on the table and I notice how puckered the whole thing is. I panic. I think, if I were a really good quilter then all the pieces would fit together perfectly and lie flat. I am forgetting that much of it is still pinned together; it will smooth and adjust as I am appliquéing. I imagine hand quilting the entire piece. I imagine the flow of the fabric that happens as space is created between each stitch. I feel the tingle in my fingers as confirmation. I can feel how the quilt becomes defined as a whole in this process. I feel the joy of anticipation. I hit the pause button and allow the joy. But the pause is short and panic appears again after a few brief moments of respite. This will take too long! How am I going to finish six pieces for this series by September if I commit to hand quilting this piece? If I devote all my spare time to this quilting, then how will everything else get done? I hit the pause button again as I consider the pleasure of finishing this quilt by hand.

Mandala Poppy, 2012

14

Mandala Poppy

The poppies in my garden in the spring of 2012 were glorious, by far the most exciting offering that year. There was something about the black center that was rich like velvet. It held potential. The black embodied a full spectrum of color but revealed itself as deep purple, like the color of spirit that moved through me when I was engaged in healing work. For a week, I would wait for the sun to come into the garden and have its brief fling with the dark centers. I took lots of close-up pictures from different angles, endeavoring to capture every illuminated fold in the velvet. The impulse to crop each photo into a square fragment of the whole resulted in my fleshing out each abstraction in fabric. Hand appliqué would be the best technique for making the undulating curves that wanted to be seen. There were nine squares. When it was time, they would all come together in a recognizable whole, a quintessential quilt top.

Photo detail of poppy

Mandala Poppy, progress detail

Each combination of red and purple offered a glimpse of this particular poppy's character, an invitation to remember the multi-faceted nature of even a single flower. Every unique fold, every juxtaposition of texture and color, was a clue to some pattern of growth that was both universal and particular at the same time. As I worked, I absorbed the uniqueness of each fragment, feeling for the essence of poppy as it emerged from the fabric and thread, enjoying the catharsis of being grounded in the task of hand appliqué.

Then I had one of those days where everything that could go wrong did, or at least it seemed that way to me at the time. The result was a lot of confrontation, self-doubt, miscommunication, tears, angst, and questioning. Everything felt like too much. Career, marriage, womanhood, motherhood, and art were the inner voices competing for attention. How could I prioritize where I channeled my love and attention?

I called my mother, expressing what felt like defeat and bitterness, and asked, "What do you think my top priority should be?" She paused and answered in a gentle voice, "For you Kathy, the top priority in your life is to be in balance." This stopped me cold in my tracks; the cynicism and negativity of the moment melted away and I knew she was right. Balance was always there for me if I looked at all the ways I expressed passion. When I followed the roots of balance in my life, they led me back to childhood family vacations in Cape Cod. This was where I experienced a perfect balance between feeling loved and finding love. These trips were always family affairs, at least the core four of us—me, my brother, mother and father— sometimes accompanied by Gramma and cousins, sometimes with family friends. We would rent a house close by my parents' oldest friends, who had made their home there, and we would all become one big family during our stay. The enduring threads of these times spent together were the beach, family fun with no time constraints, reading Nancy Drew books, and painting things on the rocks and shells I would obsessively collect. There was the thrill of antiquing, walking into a shop littered with old things, opening up a used cigar box that was full of buttons—hundreds and hundreds of buttons. I would let then sift through my fingers like treasure until I found one fashioned from mother of pearl, shimmering ivory with a hint of purple, sometimes carved with intricate designs, sometimes alone, sometimes part of a set, always evoking joy. Another time it was a box of playing cards, each card a lone representative of the pack from which it came, now living in this new place with all the other colorful characters. For years, I would look for more buttons and cards to add to each collection with no clear purpose in mind. I would feel the same thrill I felt when I rode my bike around the block after a spring thaw, finding little toys and odd lost things that had been buried under the snow and now were found. I was hunting for treasure.

Hunting for treasure allowed me to stay open to all manner of possibility that lived in creative occupation. In a world of specialists, I was a generalist who needed the freedom to explore and even master any new occupation that captured my imagination. I could only feel balance when there was no hierarchy of importance, one thing placed over another. As a young girl fascinated with the art of word and story, I read one book after another and at the same time taught myself how to do calligraphy. I would sit at my desk and practice the deft movement of hand and pen together, revealing another kind of treasure in beautiful black swirls on paper. Treasure hunting had followed me into my adult years. When Molly was old enough to have birthday parties with games, I would spend weeks designing treasure hunts for the kids, complete with maps to destinations that hid clues to where treats and toys could be found.

What treasure could I find inside this poppy? Fragments of the velvety dark center I was working were like the cards or buttons in a box. Certain combinations of color and shape distinguished themselves, captured my imagination, stopped my heart for just a moment, but for what purpose? What if I scanned my memory for the places my heart stopped to remember something precious? Would the memories be clues to why I walked so many paths simultaneously?

1. I was seven years old. My grandfather had just died. I stood at the landing of the stairs in our new house watching as my parents left for the funeral, leaving me behind. I was too young, they said. I knew the gentle man from Albania who was my grandfather cherished and adored me still. How could they know this if I didn't tell them? I would lie in bed in the dark for months after his passing, feeling him there with me. Spirit wasn't a word I could summon in my head, but it was an essence I felt, real and true. Being with Grandpa this way left me comforted and unafraid.

2. I had just moved into an apartment in Greenwich Village that would be my home for my junior year at the Institute for Architecture and Urban Studies. I was twenty years old and after weeks of looking for a summer job before classes began, was finally hired as a bartender at a joint called The Sound of Music in the theatre district of NYC. I had the day shift. I would arrive midday to find the security gate still in place, and rattle it loudly while yelling to the owner who was still sleeping inside, *Frank, come let me in*! Being a bartender was in my blood. My grandfather had owned a bar and grill in Jamestown, NY, where my father grew up, called The Wisteria Grill. Lucille Ball would hang out there when she was a young girl, just as Billie Holiday would hang out here at The Sound of Music in her day. I would walk down Broadway at the end of my shift, reveling in the richness of the day's experiences. I merged with my chosen path. I loved the idea of choosing the profession of architecture because it, like me, depended on integrating many viewpoints into one clear journey.

3. The times I remember most vividly growing up with my brother were the road trips. A movie reel of back seat adventures. For long trips, we were allowed to camp out in the wayback of the station wagon, lying down and out of sight of mom and dad, looking out the back window at sky and sun while waving at passing trucks. We would sit in the back seat with paper and pencil making up drawing games; "the silliest face"

was my favorite, winning with my one-eyed goof. Without seatbelts to constrain us, we would put our heads in each other's laps, unafraid. We would pile back into the car after a rest stop with new supplies of treats, handfuls of candy and gum, making up more new games, like who could make their fireball last the longest, or who could concoct the most unique combination of flavors in one bite. In our teenage years, it was ice cream cones, and the slow race to see who could make their cone last the longest, the winner holding a pinky sized end of cone with just a drop of ice cream. We would laugh uncontrollably, forcing our mother to turn around with stern looks and shushes, which would only make us laugh harder. We were coconspirators of pleasure and companionship. It felt completely natural.

4. I became a swimmer early in life, with summers spent at our country club pool learning to race and dive and do water ballet, as it was called then. In high school I was on the swim team. I wasn't particularly good, but I went to practice each day. I was an achiever who was not achieving in any obvious way, but I kept doing the work. Then one day it happened. We were doing sprints against each other and I was flying in the water in a way I'd never felt before. Something had clicked; my body was moving exactly the way it needed to to make me fast. Just as I was registering the exquisite feeling of gliding, I heard my teammates yelling, "*GO Kathy GO!*" They saw what I was feeling.

5. Standing on a street in the heart of downtown Rochester, NY could be a lonely affair. This part of the city had been cut off, literally wrapped in a highway that choked the small hub of stores and office buildings off from where we lived. There was the inner city inside this bubble, where the black people lived, kids who rode the bus to my school as part of the desegregation movement. It was 1974 and I was sixteen years old. As a new driver, I had braved the speeding cars and found my way to a place that felt familiar: the new Midtown Mall behind me, the historic Sibley's building across the street, and of course

the Gannett building—the walnut building to me—always gracing the skyline with its unique top. I was there to take photographs for my art class assignment. There were no people walking the streets. I gazed across the river and into the space between the two halves of the walnut building's spire and promised myself that I would live in a city where walking the streets between my home and such beauty would be a consistent part of each day.

6. I was seventeen and he was twenty-two. We met on the ski slopes by day and in a local joint at night to dance. Both were safe places. The ski slopes were in the snow belt of southwestern New York State, frequented by Americans and Canadians alike. As a family, we would make the drive early on Saturday mornings when there was snow, and we'd be the first on the slopes. He was a racing coach, and I liked to ski fast. It took only the space of a weekend skiing together and a first date to know I was going to fall for this vibrant red-headed man. I walked to the ladies' room after our first dance, the two of us moving to the same beat at the same time. As I walked through the door a voice as clear as a bell said, *you are going to fall in love with him.* It was that simple.

7. Studio art classes at my college were held in a vintage carriage house adjacent to the historic house of the art department. I spent a lot of time there as a student, and loved the solitude and space available to practice making art. One day, a friend in the advanced sculpture class told me that they were looking for a nude model to work with. "Are you interested?" I'm not sure if I said yes because I had a crush on this friend or if I just wanted to know what it would feel like to be exposed as female form objectified. My advisor was the professor for this class. His cast figures would emerge from a long process of sculpting first in clay, something he would often do right alongside his advanced students. I was curiously comfortable with the two poses that I held for very long periods of time over the course of the semester. The following year I was studying architecture in NYC and went to an art opening of

my advisor's work there. Unbeknownst to me, I had been honored in a sculpture of two reclining female nudes, the title of the piece, "Two Kathys."

8. If I had given birth to my daughter, Molly, a hundred years ago, I most likely would have died. She delivered easily enough after the insurance company was convinced to pay for the version that turned her from a breach position and set her head facing down toward the birth canal. Once she emerged, it was a flurry of happy activity to clean her up from her long stay in the womb and get her back in my arms. Carol, the comedienne midwife who did gigs on the side, was attending that day. She stood next to me tugging gently on the umbilical cord, trying to make me laugh as we waited for the placenta to be delivered. Instead, I started hemorrhaging and my routine delivery turned into a crisis. I was whisked into the OR for an emergency D&C to remove a shredded placenta and stop the bleeding. Hours later, after celebrating with champagne and family in the recovery room, after I thought that all the family was gone, I was wheeled out to a hall and lay there alone while my room was prepared. My father appeared out of nowhere and stood next to me, silent and comforting, and then finally asked, "How are you?" All I could say, feeling so profoundly supported in that moment was, "I'm so happy and I'm so hungry, what I wouldn't give for a cheeseburger!"

9. Practicing hand-piecing skills while on bedrest during my pregnancy with Ben was a perfect context for daydreaming, for feeling into a possible future where my childhood dream of being a writer could appear. I saw the novel I had always wanted to write. I imagined a livelihood that devoted half my time to quilting, half to writing, each endeavor feeding the other. For me, it would be the ultimate creative life.

When the nine blocks were finished, I began to test arrangements on the design board. I had to inset each block in another in order to complete a center that was recognizable. The inside corners were a welcome challenge, adding a depth of precision to the image that felt good. The rest of the quilt fell into place with simple rectangular pieces punctuated by a few curves, all of which could easily be machine pieced.

Even the path of marriage after divorce could produce memorable moments to integrate. My ex-husband the artist came one day to pick up our son, Ben, and while waiting, sat in front of the finished quilt top pinned up on the wall. He studied it silently and I finally had to ask, "What do you think?" He said, with as close to reverence as I'd ever heard in his voice, "I wouldn't change a thing; every single piece is exactly where it is supposed to be."

Inspired, I made finishing this quilt a priority. But I rushed it, impatience leading me to make the sweeping, curved machine-stitched lines I liked to do. Puckers and imperfections began to form. What had felt balanced now felt out of balance. Doubt gave me space to pause and wonder what the hell I was doing. Why did I fall into this work with such seriousness and joy and sense of purpose even if I didn't know what the purpose was? I came back

Mandala Poppy, detail

to the dark purple and decided to switch to quilting by hand. The question finally dissipated into the dense lines of thick stitches in the center of the poppy and brought me back to what I knew.

I was a quiltmaker. I loved quilts. I loved the entire process of making a quilt, from my initial response to a piece of fabric that calls to me, to the final stitch of sewing a binding in place. I loved the moments, viscerally felt, when the assemblage of fabric and batting and thread transcends the physical fact of construction and becomes, magically, a quilt. Moments were registered in my hands through touch and love—hands that lovingly held every cut of fabric and felt a meditative moment in every stitch. ❄

Dream Reverie

I am standing at the edge of a beach, there is a dock and a boat. Then I am in the boat in the middle of a body of water, and all of a sudden, white dolphins start leaping out of the water over the boat. They just keep coming and coming and I am overwhelmed and thrilled at the same time. One stops and takes my finger in its mouth. I am afraid at first, then relax and realize I am okay. Then there is a baby dolphin pushing its nose down my shirt, trying to get to my breasts. I realize that I have milk in my breasts; they are so full, so I squeeze some out and the baby dolphin starts drinking, then all of a sudden he turns into a little brown boy, and I have the knowledge that this little boy will be human for a while, but then grow into a great white dolphin.

Mandala Faces, 2012

15

Honor Mother

I didn't set out to make a quilt about *Mother*. It's what it became while I endeavored to capture the essence of three portraits—of me, my daughter, and my mother, all at four years old—living in oval frames that hung in hierarchical order on my parents' bedroom wall. I began by making abstract representations to align on the design wall as they appeared together where I found them. Mom, at the top, was all bouncy, smiley joy. She exuded childlike innocence and authenticity, robust, round cheek meeting toothy smile, as if all was right in the world and there wasn't anything to be afraid of. The portrait of me in the middle captured seriousness, with closed-lipped smile and quietly smiling eyes. There was something behind that smile. It said, *I know something, but I'm not telling.* Daughter Molly's portrait at the bottom was the most direct, with a piercing expression of power, defiance, and resolve so palpable as to belie her age.

At first, it wasn't clear where the expression of the feminine passed from one generation to the next might manifest in this quilt. The abstracted faces were like seeds of a ripe lineage. I didn't see the energy of the fourth face as it formed. It just happened. It was more a feeling of archetypal *Mother* that seemed to embrace all three of us in swirls of orange and blue, as if emerging from the passion of an elemental fire.

The pinned together composition was named *Mandala Faces* and came home with me from the workshop where it had begun. It occupied the design wall in my living room for months before I was ready to negotiate the final seams that needed to be made. I decided to hand appliqué the large sweeping curves instead of machine piecing them as I had done up to this point. It was a time-consuming process. I relished turning under each edge and pinning it into place. I would clear my work table, position the bulk of the quilt with pinned edge in front of me, and thoroughly enjoy the single-minded catharsis of making the small invisible stitches. My mind would follow a curve into a question.

How do you honor Mother when you think she is unsafe? When her waters become poisoned, or her love becomes obscured by violent ways? How do you forgive Mother that can't be there when you need her, when you are compelled to honor her no matter how absent she might be? How do you continue to love Mother who is simply doing the best she can, but still hurts from her own wounding? These questions were as old as time. Though there were personal aspects to all these questions, it was the universal, far-reaching, across-the-globe familiarity of all human beings struggling to honor *Mother*, pushing through with insistence.

Mandala Faces, detail

And then I would remember the feeling of reluctantly emerging from the luminous wet cave in the depths of *Mother Earth* during a meditation. The experience of finding myself in rich darkness, with just the right amount of light emanating from a crystal sphere on a stand in the center, was as real an experience as any other. I knew I was in the heart of *Mother* and I never wanted to leave. Here, she evoked mystery, depth of feeling, and knowing. She could coax the truth from me. She enveloped and contained and made sure to let me know I was loved even if I wasn't listening. She nourished and fed in the most natural of ways, pouring life into me with her watery presence. *Mother* was there, hovering in and out of the year 2012 while I continued to work slowly, meticulously sewing each curve into place. She used her considerable influence, raising my awareness of where her energy lived in me.

That summer I visited my daughter, Molly, in Peru. She was living in Cusco, working on a self-initiated internship for which she had received a sizable scholarship. All I had to do was get myself there. Traveling with a large backpack, I was looking forward to being unencumbered and letting go to the life rhythms of my accomplished daughter. I arrived with just the necessary clothing to keep me warm at night and protect me from intense sun during the day. I also brought a few things to sew with: some black squares of fabric, embroidery floss, a thread cutter, one large embroidery needle, and a square of cloth with a kantha-stitched snake I had made a few years earlier. I had no idea what I would be doing with it. I only knew I was supposed to bring it.

Molly's music teacher invited us to the christening of his year-old son. The snake was a powerful symbol of Incan spirituality. As one of the three primary holy power animals representing life and rebirth, the snake evoked the gift of life with Pachamama, Mother Earth. With absolute clarity, I saw how my stitched version of this sacred symbol could become the center of a quilt to make to give as a gift.

The first adventure out of Cusco with Molly was an overnight to Ollantaytambo in the Sacred Valley. We were squished together in the front seat of a combi, Molly practicing her Quechua with the reserved driver, who magically opened up and began to speak animatedly once he heard her address him in his native language. I was silenced as much by the beauty of watching my daughter light up with joy in her connection with another human being as I was by the breathtaking *apus* that were coming into view. The massive glaciers that lined the winding path of the Urubamba River were awe-inspiring reminders of the powerful spiritual presence of *Mother* in her most solid form.

Ollantaytambo (pronounced O-yan-tie-Tom-bo) is typically a stop on the way to Machu Picchu for most tourists, but we were going there just to be *there*. Molly needed a rest from her busy life in Cusco and I needed a first foray into the realm of Incan architecture and the Sacred Valley. The morning after our arrival, we were some of the first up into the terraces that incorporated ingeniously designed Incan canals. It was thrilling to feel the integrity of these stone constructions, to feel with every step the clear purpose of making habitable space on the side of a mountain. As we were working our way down, an older, petite woman intersected our path. I watched as she moved with agility and grace, even if guided on the arm of a younger man. I found myself watching for her white sweater and bright blue skirt, continuing to feel the energy of this woman, curious, wanting to know who she was, thinking, *I want this energy when I am her age.*

The opportunity to make contact came at the bottom of the ruins, where channels created for the flowing water began to disperse and distribute. Molly struck up a conversation with Ernesto, son of Maria Francesca. We learned that they were also here for the first time, visitors from a small town south of Cusco. We continued through the ruins together while Maria excitedly pointed out each place where she discovered water. She and I walked silently together while Molly and Ernesto chatted. I felt timeless in her presence, a companionship that resulted from being mutually in awe of the water. She led me with determination into the water temple where we stood reverently together. I dipped my hand in the clear, cold, rushing water of the river to which all the channeled streams outside flowed, and like a little kid, she grinned, knelt down, and did the same. *Honor Mother.* It was a complete thought that encompassed a feeling so much bigger than I could contain in that moment, taking in all the spirits of mothers and daughters and grandmothers that hold the flow of her, of Mother Earth, Pachamama, in our very souls. Maria Francesca took off her broad brimmed hat and stood there beaming in her joy.

Later in the afternoon, Molly and I climbed up the mountain on the other side of town to a place that gave a clear view out over the winding snake of the Urubamba River and the Sacred Valley beyond. We sat together, mother and daughter, and reflected on being strong, independent women who venture into uncharted waters.

Meanwhile, the search for material with which to make the quilt became a daily activity. Cotton cloth was a rare commodity in Peru. Just about all fabric was woven from wool or synthetic fibers of some sort, in bright colors and designs characteristic of the region. It took days for me to realize that everything I was finding—mostly mass-produced on factory looms with synthetic yarns—was made in the spirit of traditionally hand-woven pieces. They would have to do.

With Molly in charge, I could easily surrender to her passion for the culture of historic Cusco built on top of a mountain. It didn't matter that quilt-making wasn't a tradition here. She indulged me, filtered my desire to make this quilt through her own ability to follow a vision in a foreign culture. She bargained for me at a stall in the large public market, for some spools of thread, needles, and a large pair of scissors. She led me to her favorite vendors in search of inexpensive, tightly woven scarves and wraps that I could use as fabric. In the early morning while she slept, I would cut rectangular pieces and cautiously sew them together one by one, hoping that the stitches would hold the various weaves together. In this way each day began, the fabric combining with the glow of time spent with my precious daughter.

It was a happy day when I discovered bolts of flannel-like cotton in bright, solid colors at another huge public market; I purchased several pieces to work into the design. It was as if the orange and blue and red of the quilt I had left at home to be finished had followed me here. With a growing stash of fabric, my daily design choices and engagement with the developing quilt expanded exponentially. I now had a purpose and a focus while walking the streets, and a place to put my heart and

Peru quilt, 2012

hands during the morning hours I spent alone.

I could have viewed the bulky hand-sewn seams as clumsy. It would have been easy to judge the whole endeavor as beneath the standard of artistry and craftsmanship I had grown accustomed to. But my years as a dedicated quilter were serving me well. I didn't worry about a thing. I thoroughly enjoyed the process and the challenge of completing a baby quilt in time for the christening. The batting became a single layer of white flannel, and the back was fashioned out the rest of the colored flannel, folded over and blind stitched in place to form the binding after all three layers were tied together with black embroidery floss. In ten days' time, it was done.

Like all the quilts I had made before this and all the quilts made since, the improvisational quality of the work led me into the awe I felt each day. It was no coincidence that the snake was there guiding the way, helping me shed whatever limitations I thought there might be and to complete this task with nothing less than joy. It also reminded me of my power, and how to tread cautiously on this earth in a quest for beauty and accomplishment.

A week following our trip to Ollantaytambo, Molly and I went to Machu Picchu. We hiked up to the Sun Gate, the place where the Inca trail ends and the first glimpse of this famed city on top of the mountain can be seen. The rock steps were steep and I was moving very slowly, already feeling the effects of the climb under the hot Andean sun at 7:30 in the morning. I felt tears rising and falling inside of me with each step, which occasionally did spill out in full expression. Molly was confused by my tears. I explained that they were happy tears, spontaneous tears, necessary tears, tears that were accompanied by two very clear words each time I felt the tide ... *Honor Mother* ...

We arrived at the Sun Gate as the city of Machu Picchu became very small behind us. The waves of emotion I continued to feel gave way to the relief of being able to rest in this new perch and bask in the delight of being where we were. As I settled in I heard the rush of water, unmistakable, and yet there was no source for this in sight. We finally realized we were sitting on a hidden pipe or channel that was running right underneath us, a clear strong voice, reminding us of the significance of *Mother's* flowing presence even in this lofty place.

The christening was a glorious day of celebration in both Christian and Peruvian style. And while the Christian ceremony only took an hour, the Peruvian celebration was an all-day affair, weaving together people and food and music and dance and gift giving. I sat at a long table with women of many generations who showed me, without words, how to honor the food we were sharing. I took my place in the circle that surrounded the baby, waiting my turn to place my gift at his feet, in honor of Pachamama.

Molly finding her way to this sacred land felt like an affirmation of the way *Mother* had been working through the four generations of women I was part of. Even though Gramma had just passed, her love of travel to exotic places on earth and the sheer pleasure she derived from putting her bare hands into the earth somehow found root in the next generations. At the age of fifty-five, my mother discovered her love of nature in a week long Outward Bound wilderness course. There in the wilds of Maine, she fell in love with her strength and resolve to survive. The experience propelled her to look for land and home in the hills near her house, where her relationship to tree and rock and water could be constant and immediate.

I began to understand how *Mother* had been speaking to me about natural law all along in my dreams. She was bringing me back to the core in me that would always find joy in making connection, in how my fluid body cycled with the moon and the tides and the dolphins and the emotions of my loved ones. This path led me out of a dedicated urban lifestyle into small-town living and eventually into the sacred land that I had just spent the better part of two years sharing with a lover. The relationship with the man ended, but my relationship to *Mother* and her vast terrain had just begun. ❈

Reverie

What if I combine the leftover cooked sweet potatoes from Christmas Eve dinner with the leftover brown rice from two nights ago? What if I mash the potato, add the rice and an egg, form patties, and fry them in some olive oil? Add some salt and cayenne pepper to the mix. Preheat the pan and put the patties in and stand there to keep watch, imagining the crunchy exterior forming now, careful, don't want them to burn, turn them in the pan just in time, oh dear, are they burned? No. Just a little darker than I imagined. While they continue to slowly brown on the other side, fire on low, I prepare the head of fresh broccoli, cut it into small pieces that will cook in just moments in a pan with equal splashes of water, olive oil, tamari and lemon juice for steaming until just crisp done. It doesn't feel like there are any more questions, the stream of "what ifs" has combined to form a clear process that results in a plate arranged with two patties and the broccoli heaped across the middle and sprinkled with sesame seeds.

Delicious. Simple and satisfying. The small amount of potato-rice mix left in the bowl is formed into one last patty for the pan. It is no longer a question or a mystery as to how long it will take to brown evenly, and this one last patty is seemingly perfect, so what is left to question here if I were to make it again? Only everything! Is it an organic potato? What kind of sweet potato? Where was it grown? What kind of brown rice, short grain or long grain? Where does the olive oil come from, does it matter? What kind of pan is used, would it make a difference if it was a non-stick pan instead of the stainless steel one I used? Is it sea salt or regular salt with iodine? Does any of this really make a difference?

I know I will never make this dish exactly the same way again. I know that I have loved making it. And I know that even the best recipe that has been used over and over again is an illusion at best, that the recipe is simply a guide to experiencing, in awareness, a moment of unique ingredients, particular atmosphere, and energy from the hands and heart that have prepared.

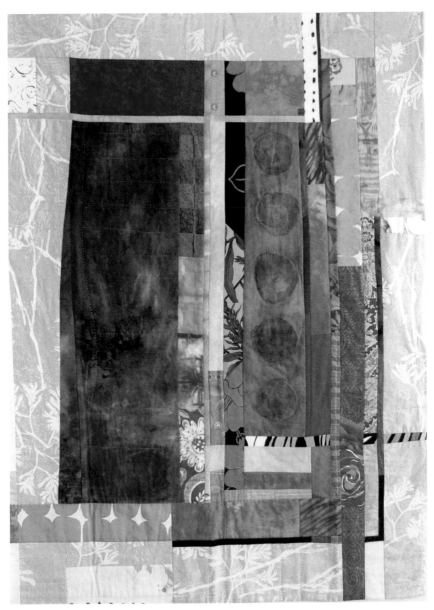

Scrap #1, 2015

16

Spontaneous Accomplishment

I started writing a blog called *Spontaneous Accomplishment* in the fall of 2011. While it was inspired by the relatively small acts of creativity I experienced in the kitchen every day in relation to what was going on in my life at the time, it wasn't long before the joy of seeing connection on a daily basis began to include all the ways I experienced creative spirit moving through me. From Buddhist lore, I understood spontaneous accomplishment to be the potentiality inherent in emptiness, form never separate from emptiness and emptiness never separate from form. I wanted to believe that all things already existed in emptiness and that the natural state of mind is one where *everything* could be accomplished without effort. It was a worthy path to follow if I wanted to live free of the suffering that comes on the heels of expectation.

That fall I was gifted three large plastic bags of fabric scraps. I emptied the bags on the floor and gathered everything into one big mound, then added the pile of scraps sitting on top of my sewing table. I pulled out the large storage bin, also completely full of scraps. All together it was an impressive amount of fabric and quite overwhelming. I didn't want to throw any of it away. I was aiming for a clean slate, one that would allow me to see the fabric in a different way so I could actually use it. I needed a different kind of discerning process. I began to iron wrinkled, bunched-up pieces and notice casual and random combinations where pieces landed when I was finished. I began to imagine a whole series of quilts that could be made from these scraps.

One of my favorite practices is to close my eyes, run my hand across my bookshelf, and blindly choose *or be led to* a book. Or, while looking for something specific, another book will catch my eye and attention, and I'll take that one instead, flip through the pages, and randomly open to a page and read. I always trust that a message is there, that something I am supposed to see and take in is contained in this random finding. Sometimes what is there is so potent and poignant that I have to make a record of it, typing each word onto a new page to feel the meaning more deeply. Often it will be whole pages' worth in order to capture every last drop, diligently copied and recorded to be discovered in this new context at another time. I began a similar process of randomly selecting, pressing and cutting, and sewing these scrap pieces of fabric into strips, working very quickly, combining pieces together from the growing pile on my sewing work table with flashes of guiding intuition.

I was aware that my work had moved from traditionally patterned quilt designs to an inspired way of working through improvisation, which created lots of scraps. I had my way. But I was feeling the pull to change my mind about what this process had to be, to not be tethered to a recipe for any kind of success. The yogi in me, who valued embodied awareness as a prerequisite for creative growth, was sure there were multiple paths to improvisation. The work was to create context for this to happen continuously.

When I first started quilting, my entire fabric stash was small enough to live in a few drawers and boxes. Saved scraps from this meager collection were the afterthoughts, easily forgotten. By the time we moved to Massachusetts, the expanded stash, now complete with its own small scrap box, moved into an armoire in my bedroom while the adjacent walk-in-closet-sized room received a carpet and became my dedicated yoga practice space. Within a year, a sewing table moved in and I put up a design wall, satisfied that I still had enough room for yoga practice. But it wasn't long before the fabric, feeling the sacredness of this room, asked to come out of the closet and be relocated there, too. Walls were filled with open shelving for the fabric to live on, and my practice here shifted full time to quiltmaking.

As the collection of fabric grew and things began to get messy with more stock to work with, more scraps, and more uncertainty about how my life was changing in relation to divorce and single motherhood, I moved my red meditation cushion back in to re-establish much-needed ground in daily practice. The room and the fabric that lived here continued to provide me with a stable place that felt safe. But then even that began to change. The fabric wanted a new place to take its sacred charge. I rearranged the furniture in the living room and made space for a new dedicated quilting corner, right next to my beloved fireplace. And though I knew bringing it into the heart of my home might be a welcome change, there was daily life to compete with here, and not enough room for everything to be in view. The fabric was lovingly arranged by color in flat stackable baskets that could live out of sight under the sewing table, and everything remained neat and tidy in its new place, unseen.

It wasn't long before the fabric began to call to me to come out of hiding. In a single impulsive afternoon, I loaded all the baskets into the back of my car and drove them out to my new love's home and into the sacred room above the separate barn that we slept in during the hot summer months. It was exhilarating to be able to arrange these baskets in a way that captured the shifting light of the day and the cool mountain breeze. Yet as beautiful as the fit seemed to be, it soon became clear that the fabric was not happy here; it never really felt enough at home to leave the safety of the baskets, never really got to make the creative mess it was used to making. The problem was that it was hard to get up to this space, through a hole in the floor with a glorified ladder. I designed a stair and began to dream about how to make this space more accessible, but it was too much of a struggle to get it built. The relationship ended that had brought me here. And so the fabric was loaded back up into the car and deposited back onto the floor in a big pile in the center of my home. Something major needed to shift. In another swirl of spontaneity, all the books that lived on the ample shelves were boxed up and given away and the fabric moved back in, tantalizingly accessible and visible from its seat in the heart of where I truly lived.

My home context was in transition during this time. I was preparing to sell the house. The spare bedrooms were now occupied by international graduate student boarders. We shared the public rooms, and now that my studio was set up in a corner of the living room, quiltmaking time was shared with the frequent presence of those eating or working at the dining table. Everything was in view, work in progress on the wall, sewing machine like a table ornament, the built-in bookshelves filled with the entirety of my fabric stash, filling the room with color and texture.

The next two years passed in this new arrangement. The house was a bustle of tenants moving in and out, Ben graduating from high school and moving to his new school in the next town, Molly graduating from college and moving to Peru. During this time, our family dog, Yankee, passed and we adopted a new puppy. I began to take puppy Nora to a community conservation area where dogs could be off leash. We would go early to share the rising sun and the hush of morning with the woods. It would seem like we were the only life, moving along trails that led us deeper into woods or up the mountain for a spectacular view of the valley below. In these woods, I had been sharing with others (tree and human alike) about selling the house and changing my life. Change. Another one of those words that held the potential for suffering and growth in the emptiness between what was and what would be. Change was getting to the end of a path and watching Nora go one way while saying, *No, we're going the other way this morning*, and feeling the ease that comes with gratitude as she looked at me with tilted head and cocked an ear before turning 180 degrees and trotting in the direction of the *other way*.

The light on the trail was more precise one morning, as if to reinforce the knowledge that change in my life would take a focused path unfolding exactly the way it was supposed to. I was amazed at the feeling of both grace and anxiety as Nora and I approached the last stretch of the trail that ran along the brook and were met by Sam and his human, Abby, Maggie and Ruby and their human, Brett, and a little further down, Miss Darcy and her human. We stood around and chatted as the dogs frolicked. In just one month I had become part of a whole new community in a place I loved. Like my scraps of fabric, the episodic and unpredictable quality of encounters here in this place each day had brought me into a new experience of intimacy with others. I never knew when we would encounter other dogs and their humans. I had to learned to trust how Nora would respond to them. The potential for community was always there. I began writing about these heartfelt (even if transitory) connections I felt each morning, and shared them with an anonymous world of blog readers on the internet.

I was also learning how to share an intimacy of experience in my own home with non-family members. Working on my quiltmaking in the open with nothing hidden was new. I wasn't removed or isolated from my daily life as I typically would be in retreat. I completed the first quilt from my scraps working this way, and called it *Scrap 1*. I suspended all doubt and trusted

Scrap #2, progress detail

that where I was in any moment was exactly where I was supposed to be. I witnessed order and character emerging, knowing it would inform in some way the structure of how the next quilt would develop. I began sewing together the scraps of the scraps to become the center of a next quilt, *Scrap 2.* It was just the same as what happened in the kitchen as I gathered ingredients that were right there in that moment, making something delicious with scraps of food. I was enjoying the cathartic and peaceful quality of allowing myself to be led.

Scrap #2, 2013

It wasn't about frugality. I loved the process of using scraps of scraps. It was the curve of the spiral of sustainability that led me to intersect with community that I had come to love. The very act of using and reusing and recombining in new ways was exactly what brought me back the essence of something coexisting with the unknown. How long would it take me to use all the scraps of my scraps moving forward? Where would this motivation engage with the rest of my fabric stash, and where would I feel the pull to purchase or make something new to complete an impulse or vision?

Scrap 2 was finished and out in the world long before I moved with Nora to my new home in the country in 2014. The entire living room of the antique post-and-beam house I now lived was devoted to quiltmaking. I kept *Scrap 1* in sight but it was months before I began to work on it again. Even though it had been quilted together with invisible machine-quilted lines in the ditch (that is, the actual seam where two pieces of fabric meet) and it was technically a completed quilt, it was still unfinished in my mind, more like an abstract painting, devoid of the characteristic texture and character of visible quilted pattern. I had begun three different hand quilted designs, chalked lines and curves to follow with thick thread and visible stitches that all eventually got ripped out. I kept coming back to a feeling of square one. As if coming back could initiate a glimpse of another way. I was discovering the simple pleasures of living in the country and moving to a completely different rhythm. I would walk the woods with Nora each day, experiencing a range of breath and peace I didn't know was possible. Bringing this sensibility to a quilt that had started in another life was a challenge. The quilt embodied history that wanted to be honored and it embodied history that also wanted to be finished.

It was humbling to still be pining for a truly beloved spool of thread. It was thread I had dyed myself in a workshop years before, and I was thrilled with the result. There was something just perfect in the weight, feel and variegated color of this thread that continued to call to me through the years, the shades of blues, greens, and purples that added a kind of shimmer and depth to each of the three quilts it graced. Three full spools of this thread had translated into countless hours of hand-quilted stitches. I wished I had more of this thread to finish the quilt. There was no other thread that could come close to producing the effect I thought I wanted, yet another reason not to finish the quilt.

One day, I felt the call to move deeper into the woods I had been exploring with Nora, walking what seemed to be a trail between two stone walls. As isolated as we were, I felt the presence of human intervention here; someone built those walls. Deeper in, the walls became even more present, configured in a way that suggested more than just a boundary or an edge. There were so many of them. Was this the site of a single person, a family, or a whole community? My mind began to fill in the gaps between the questions and I got it: this land was once true wilderness for whatever inhabitants had been there. But even with the silence and the reclamation of the earth sending it back to what it must have been before this intervention, I still didn't feel wilderness. Not yet. As I continued on the path, there was a point where complete silence was met with a sense of complete unknown. This was the tipping point, the edge where I felt the sense of something wholly other than human. I thought of the bobcat that had been found dead on the road nearby recently. That animal had surely lived in these woods. There was a flash of the barest hint of fear of lurking predators as I thought of what was ahead. My pace slowed to a stop in anticipation of turning around; I thought, *this is far enough*. But the flash swirled away and I forged ahead. So this was wilderness. I marveled at the organization of this natural world, vine art, fungus beauty, rock comfort, tree spirit, and clear, reflective water. I was completely at the mercy of where I was. Like pushing a reset button, I could begin again right here, in whatever mental, emotional, physical, or spiritual space I happened to be occupying at the moment. I felt safe. And though I could be the only human that had ever been there, I knew this wasn't true. Fire and food and art and civilization and more thread were, after all, just around the corner.

The next day I came back to *Scrap 1*. It had been sustaining a slow burn all this time. I had been smothering the piece with the desire for more quilting than was necessary with thread that was gone. Finally, I was able to step back and allow the same economy of improvisation that inspired the quilt in the first place to inform its completion. I saw simple lines that needed to be marked, like a code that floated out of the great blue space of fabric. The stitches accentuating the swirls in the most minimal way were almost invisible, like the stitching in the ditch that had already been there doing its work for so many years.

I had made simple pieces in the past but never believed in their value because they took such a short time to complete. As if belaboring something and then forcing a design or an idea to meet a deadline had value. Now I was regarding a finished quilt that, for all intents and purposes, took five years to complete. Its value could not be measured in time. I could finally change my mind. Less may be more, but the time it took to get there was priceless. In the emptiness where all form lived, there was no time. Five years might as well have been five blinks of an eye. ✸

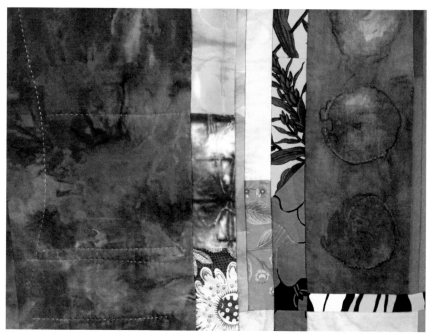

Scrap # 1 detail

Reverie

I stand at the ironing board with a handful of stray pieces of fabric just pulled out of the big scrap bin kept under my sewing table. Ironing scraps is cathartic. I love the feel of color and the vibration of an otherwise isolated and lonely piece. As each scrap becomes wrinkle free, I lay it out on the right side of the ironing board, ends draping over the edges. The collection soon becomes a gathering and I finally take notice of what is forming. It is a beautiful rectangular—almost square—arrangement. It wants to be honored in some way. I carefully slide my hands underneath to pick up the entire assembly and carry it over to an unoccupied end of the dining room table. The edge of a curve announcing itself as part of a circle distinguishes itself. The vision of four blocks forms, each carrying a section of this circle. The awareness of being with the presence of something truly divine moves with my breath, my heart beating loudly with the recognition of companionship. Exhaling presents a new moment to consider and I have to decide to leave or stay. Before the vision can fade, I pin the pieces of fabric together where they are, go to iron some more, and quickly frame out the four blocks that will eventually come together in a circle for a new square quilt. There will be gaps to fill and more to discover. Seeing structure emerge this way is as elusive and as unpredictable as a gust of wind. Once seen however, I can fully commit, settle in, and move toward a completed moment. Once felt, I can continue to move toward what is there in my heart.

Seeing Wind Mandala, 2015

17

Seeing Wind

It had been days since Yankee and I had been out for a walk. The beautiful Golden Retriever puppy that had become our family dog had seen me through changes—from life with young kids through separation and divorce, and now, as an empty-nester, into a more solitary existence. He had spent much of his thirteen years alone in the house during the days while we were at work and school. A mellow, quiet, soulful presence, he would eventually demand time outside to connect with the world in some way. When he asked to go out, I either waited at the door to let him back in when he was finished with his business, or tied him to his lead so he could lie on the warm pavement in the sun on the driveway, like a lion marking the threshold to home, head up to catch the wind blowing through his rich, golden fur. If I wasn't at the door when he returned, he would simply leave, wandering the neighborhood and the town. This always resulted in a call from a knowing neighbor who had detained him, or from the police with news of the kind soul who has taken him in. When Yankee took off like that, my heart would lodge in my throat. At some level, I knew he was fine and would be taken care of, that he needed to feel his independence and freedom. I wanted to believe that my love was enough to bring him home. At another level, I felt irresponsible and neglectful and worried. The leash and the lead were just other names for tether, and I hated that I had to use them all these years, aware of how this tether might be inextricably linked to Yankee's behavior.

Our walks always began with me clipping on the leash at the door. We moved fast, and Yankee was always as many paces ahead as the leash would allow. He was so beautiful. And even at thirteen years old, his gait was brisk with eager bounce in each step. We were walking past the track at the high school which abutted open fields. There wasn't a soul in sight and in a flash of inspiration, I unclasped the leash and he took off like a shot, running with focus and abandon. He would then lag behind for a stretch, and as I called to him, he would run full speed past me to set the lead again. This pattern continued until we arrived at the point where I needed to put the leash back on. He came right to me, no argument, his breathing hard and fast. I swear he was smiling.

As we walked the last stretch home, I wondered why it had taken me so long to test the waters with Yankee in this way. Maybe I was the one who had been conditioned by the tether all those years. I desperately wanted to change my mind. I believed that never properly training Yankee had left him unpredictable and noncompliant. But now, as long as I could be present with him, simply coexist in spirit with him during his moments of freedom and joy, he would come back when it was time. The tether no longer felt like a tether right then, but rather a commitment to truly pay attention.

We arrived at the end of the private dirt road leading to our house and I let him off the leash again. He raced to the front yard with playful leaps, looking for the bone that was hiding there. I watched him from the kitchen window, his energy youthful and palpable. I called to him through the glass and he looked straight at me with a challenging expression. He sniffed at a gust of wind and settled down right onto the ground where he was. He continued looking at me with a gaze turned wise and intense. What I heard was, *I am out here but I am not alone, and neither are you.* Until that moment, feeling alone had not been a conscious thought.

Just a few weeks later Yankee wandered off. My effort to communicate and bring him home with my heart failed and I barely slept that night, disconnected from the love I had been taking for granted for so many years. The call came from the police the next morning. A neighbor had found him in the wee hours, hungry and weak. He actually collapsed as we began our walk home together. It was a turning point for Yankee. After some food and rest he returned to his quiet stoic way of taking care of himself, but he was never quite the same. His movements visibly slowed. He seemed to be sliding a little bit each day into the dark calm that would eventually claim him in death.

During this time, I continued to work on the new quilt. I machine pieced whatever could be sewn in an obvious way, even the tricky inside corners and curves. But the interconnecting tissue of this quilt would ultimately demand the slow precision of hand appliqué. The flow of finding the structure that would bind the four sections together became a kind of meditation. It required the recognition of a moment and acting on the impulse to fix it in place. The fluidity of hand appliqué allowed for subtle change while sewing, making it easier to let go of the illusion that I was maintaining something solid or fixed. Doing hand appliqué also eliminated the complication of figuring out how to get the whole assembly under a sewing machine needle. It was a pleasurable process, each stitch holding a world of anticipation. I didn't rush. The quilt top remained up on a portable design wall for weeks as my attention shifted to accommodate the grief that was developing in the space of Yankee's imminent departure.

Yankee transitioned into a form of home hospice care early that fall of 2013. He died peacefully as the leaves started coming to the ground. He was the last of my core family to leave home, and the first to leave this life. His absence highlighted a gaping hole in my awareness of what it might feel like to live in relation to just me. He left me staring into the depth of a belief that if I was alone, not visibly connected to another beating heart, I wasn't loved. I remember standing in the living room just a few feet from the spot where Yankee passed, noticing an impulse to fill the hole again. But after only a few days, the hole expanded into a palpable sense of relief at seeing this belief for what it was. I was not the center of the universe after all. It was at that moment that Nora made her presence known for a second time. I'd actually seen her three-month-old puppy face with beckoning eyes first, weeks before Yankee died, in an internet picture from her foster home. My heart leaped now as I saw her face again, noting that she was a rescue dog in need of a permanent home. It was as if Yankee were there with her, reaching out to me saying, *I am out here but I am not alone, and neither are you.* I simply didn't question the feeling of destiny that she was finding me. Ten days later, puppy Nora arrived on my doorstep.

In the spring of 2014, after years of cycling in and out of desire to let go of the past, I finally decided to put the house on the market. My real estate agent asked me one simple question: "Where are you going?" I had no answer for her.

During the months of waiting for the house to sell, I finished the quilt top, added batting and backing, and prepared it for final quilting. Nora and I began hiking the trails in a conservation area along a beautiful brook and through woods to granite ledges and breathtaking views. It took only a week of exploring and feeling the huge freedom of being with Nora this way for me to settle into an exciting awareness of how life could change. We were in the most natural form of relationship. The anxiety that she had come to me with seemed to dissipate in the wilderness. I trusted her to come when I called and I could completely relax into the energy of where I was in relation to her. Each day we would step into another world of morning as if transitioning into a fairyland. The warm rising sun was replaced by cool shaded hush and the sparkle of filtered light on water. The sounds of forest birdsong and bubbling brook would come into focus, enveloping me in a space that was as different from the moment before as my slowing gait was from Nora's enthusiastic leaping. I didn't want to take such providence for granted. What if we couldn't get here for some reason?

I would more often than not choose to "do the circle" that led partway up the mountain, across the ridge, and back down again to join the path where this particular loop began. Moving in a circle that way dispelled the illusion that there would be any kind of back-tracking. It wasn't that I couldn't open to going off the circle and exploring tangents. It was just that I had a history of feeling considerable stress from resisting any form of backtracking. I could hear my ex-husband's chuckle now, as if he were reading this, at my admission to what was a relentless need to keep moving forward no matter what, and the strain this had placed on our marriage.

I came to the conceptual starting point for the loop that had structured my imagination that morning. It was still early with no constraint of time and worry. Each step was gently felt and heard. It didn't matter if I was walking fast or slow. It didn't matter how far away Nora went because she always came back. We continued the next section of the loop up. And instead of turning to follow the ridge when I arrived there, I simply continued climbing. The path quickly became a typical mountain path of rocky ledge. I felt the welcome stretch in the back of my legs and the impulse to keep moving forward. Nora continued to do her thing, racing in and out of the woods. But she was also slowing down now, staying just a bit longer on the narrowing path that seemed to be leading us to the top of something. The sun beckoned and the promise of a clearing enticed. It would have been so easy to keep going until we reached that place. I had nothing but time. And then, just like that, I felt the impulse to turn around and go back. So simple. No agonizing or fuss, just moving in the opposite direction again. Backtracking. The swirling warmth in my chest expanded to include the beauty of Nora on the path in front of me. She had taken to stopping and waiting for me, watching, sometimes even turning around and walking up to meet me. I felt the tears of acceptance in my throat, the truth of the timelessness of going off the circle, the love that was there for me to know. Soon enough we would begin to encounter the others, humans and their dogs that shared this space with us each morning. The meet and greet began just as we finished the loop, and eventually we made our way across the threshold into the bright sun again. I could go off on as many tangents as I needed to and know that I could return right *here*.

I now had an answer for my real estate agent. I wanted all this.

One of the highlights when visiting Molly in Peru had been a day to explore on my own. I had asked a young woman sitting next to me on the bus one day about sites close to Cusco I could visit by myself. When she heard that I was an architect she exclaimed, "You have to go to Tipón!" She managed to convey that it was a famous hydrological site, an engineering feat, east of the city. Molly knew nothing about this place. It was a mystery. We asked around and got a little more information and determined which bus I needed to take to get there. Not speaking any Spanish, I was at the mercy of strangers every step of the way. I was dropped off at the side of the road with no instructions at all as to how to get to Tipón. I had to negotiate a ride in the back compartment of a station wagon filled with a family also going to the site. Hiking the steep, challenging path that led to an entrance in the middle of the mountain, passing and greeting others working their way up, I realized that I was the only American there. Unlike the more famous sites to the west along the Sacred Valley that were heavily visited by tourists from all over the world, here I was amongst a small group of local Peruvians spending a day at one of their own national treasures. I was befriended by a family and sat with them sharing crackers and soda, communicating through hand gestures and smiles, warmed by being included so generously.

I spent hours meandering around by myself taking in the grand scale and ingenuity of this engineering feat: huge, wide green terraces framed on either side with stone channels and steps, one of which still carried water from somewhere further up the mountain to the town below. Just as I was leaving, I saw the map at the exit indicating that there were other ruins higher up above the terraces. It was already early afternoon and though it felt like time to go back to Cusco, I was compelled to go back up into the terraces to find the barely discernible start of a stone path to these ruins. I passed several groups on their way down. I'd periodically turn around and see the huge terraces diminishing in size, still dotted with tourists moving about. I arrived at the modest ruins and realized I was the only one there. I walked the site slowly in the silence, came to the highest point where I could command an almost perfect three-hundred-and-sixty-degree view, and stood suspended in time.

I loved the perspective of the terraces coming back into view as I descended. As I stepped off the path and scanned the vast terrain, there wasn't a soul in sight. Not one single person. Not even a dog, and dogs roamed freely everywhere in Peru. I was completely alone. I walked down to stand at the top ledge of the uppermost terrace in reverence. I knew I was having this moment for a reason that I couldn't fathom. Filled with awe, I walked around to the water altar constructed just below this uppermost terrace. Heart in throat, I honored the sacredness of the moment and then, not able to bear the solitude a moment longer, continued on down the mountain to find a ride back to Cusco.

Discovering a new world while hiking with Nora evoked a similar feeling of reverence. She had become my benchmark, the presence that anchored me to my steps and allowed me to open fully to the trees and sky and sun and water and stone in a way that felt as exhilarating as her eager pace.

When I moved to my new home in Worthington, I was quite sure it was because Nora had led me there.

Now, I stand at the top edge of a large meadow that separates the house from woods and brook beyond and I am never alone. I walk the vast terrain of wildlife management lands that abut my property and I am never alone. I was never alone in the boldness of my move to this new home in the country. It didn't take me long to settle in and begin the hand-quilted stitching that would give voice to where I was. The tight concentric circles that began off center eventually began to expand and move in alignment with the form of the circle that lived in this quilt. The quilting stitches became the core energy of this piece, holding

Seeing Wind Mandala detail

a sense of the inevitable for me, and making the quilt truly come alive. It was a profoundly intimate experience, hands moving with the wave of thread weaving in and out of fabric. Late one night, about six months after moving, I finally put the completed quilt up on the wall. How would I bind the edges? I stared at the image for a while like an objective observer seeing it for the first time, and went to bed feeling something familiar that I couldn't name.

Nora and I took a long walk deep into the woods of my neighborhood the next morning. It was a gray day with swiftly moving clouds and the sound of wind marking our progress. The whistle and swirl of tree tops swaying soon became the rhythm guiding my pace. It was a sound way out there and, at the same time, vibrating through branches and trunks down to roots deep in the earth and back up into my body. It was such a sacred sound, poignant in a way that made me want to start swaying, too. It had been like this for as long as I could remember.

The sound of wind in the woods always evoked the swirl of something deep in my belly and anchored me before settling in my heart.

At the pond, I watched the water rippling in this wind too. No amount of waiting to capture the swaying of tree branches with a camera could yield such clarity. As if it wasn't enough to see the wind blowing across the water in one direction, a gust from another direction registered its presence perfectly, as if wings on the current, ready to take off.

I was seeing wind.

Arriving home, I looked up into the sound whirling through the wide berth of sky above the meadow and saw two hawks riding the airstream of wind that was blowing there, too. They were dipping and soaring like the elegant gliders they were born to be. Gazing at the quilt now waiting on the wall, I realized that the familiarity I had gone to sleep with also lived in the outstretched wings of a hawk in the cross current of air moving across the face of the quilt. I was free. I would finish it with a faced edge, letting the image settle just as it was.

With this recognition and the next inhale of breath, the telltale swirl in my body began again. ❊

Quilt in process

Epilogue: A Quiltmaker's Way

Spring arrives, and I am seduced by the vibrant flow of water in the brook and the way in which the woods come alive to its sound and smell and touch. I want to contain the essence of this cold fluid that warms my heart. I begin making blocks of recombined strips from single pieces of fabric that evoke a sense of flow. The resultant blocks come together following a spiral of golden mean proportions, making space for more as it grows. The assemblage completed while I was still making fires in the fireplace falls into the space created by this swirl of spring contained. As the season progresses, I am able to penetrate deeper and deeper into the woods with each passing day and celebrate where water is now liberated and flowing freely on the ground. Sun illuminates movement as undulating shimmers over the decomposing debris. The quilt is finished with a sea of waves, machine-made free-form lines shimmering in a similar way, from one curve to the next and back, changing direction and color at the thin boundary between one space and another.

Now my focus shifts to swelling buds forming on trees as I take in the promise of the season upon us. The inspiration I feel for expressing what is here in this moment is limitless. Anticipation and pleasure merge, and I head inside to embrace the fabrics and threads calling to me.

Acknowledgements

The long thread of gratitude I feel begins with my core writing group. For almost five years we have come together once a month to share yearnings, inspiration, and camaraderie. Their feedback has been invaluable, as has been their support and encouragement to keep writing these chapters. Katherine, Paul, Beth, Jane, Liesel, and Mark, I can't thank you enough.

I thank:

Carolyn Crump, Jean Stearns, and my mother Ginny Ford for many enthusiastic manu-script readings and helping me know there is a place in the world for this book.

Linda McCullough Moore and the many wonderful writers I have shared stories with in her workshop gatherings.

Libby Maxey for the superb editing experience, Lisa Thompson for her graphic design expertise, and Steve Strimer for his dedication to bringing quality printing to the publishing world.

Eugen Baer, of Hobart & William Smith Colleges, professor extraordinaire, for creating the context to support my quest to 'discover order,' and for his encouragement to keep seeking.

Every cherished friend, for being there, and for asking.

And last but not least, Kathy Doughty, friend of almost fifty years, fellow co-conspirator in the joy of quiltmaking. ❋

About the Author

Kathy Ford grew up in Rochester, New York, graduated from Hobart & William Smith Colleges in 1980 with a major in design theory, and moved to New York City to pursue a career in architecture.

She received her Masters in Architecture from Harvard University in 1985 and has been practicing architecture in New York and Massachusetts for the past thirty years. She has a long history of working with local non-profit community organizations to design affordable housing in existing and historic buildings.

Her life as a quilter began shortly after becoming a mother in 1991.

Kathy currently lives with her two dogs in the hilltowns of western Massachusetts, where she devotes daily work to quiltmaking, writing, home-steading, and maintaining her architecture practice. As a passionate seeker, her explorations in holistic health and spirituality have included mothering a child with special needs, training in energy medicine, yoga, and Continuum. She began writing her blog spontaneousaccomplishment in 2011, providing inspiration for the en-deavor of seeing and feeling connection.

Kathy's quilts have been exhibited in juried shows and sold to private collections. Her body of work can be seen at **kathyford.net.** ❊